FAITH OF OUR FATHERS

OVER ONE HUNDRED OF THE OLDEST, MOST HISTORIC CHURCHES IN GEORGIA

A PICTORIAL HISTORY

By Don Joiner

To Molly + Taylor
all my love
Don Joiner

Table of Contents

Churches Listed by County

Preface

Several years ago I was surprised to learn that there was no single publication devoted to describing and portraying the earliest, still standing church buildings in Georgia. During the following two years I traveled throughout the state identifying and photographing a number of these buildings constructed before 1865, the year that brought to a close the terrible battles of the Civil War. For the most part I was guided to these buildings by the text of historic markers associated with many of them.

In 2007 Antebellum Churches in Georgia was published. This book consisted of a short history and black and white photos of a number of church buildings of that era. Although I knew that there had to be other churches of that era that were not included in the book, a number of those who purchased Antebellum Churches in Georgia suggested the names of individual churches they thought might have been constructed before 1865. Some also suggested that color photographs of these historic structures would significantly enhance the interest of the reader.

So I set out again following the directions kindly given to me by these good readers and found that indeed there were a number of additional church buildings that met the criteria of having been constructed before the end of the Civil War but were not identified by historic markers. I should point out, however, that in the course of investigating these structures I have found that it is a far simpler task to determine the year a specific congregation was formed than it is to verify the actual date of construction of the existing building.

In this new publication, *Faith of Our Fathers,* the reader will find historical background and color photographs of over one hundred of the oldest, most historic churches still standing in the state of Georgia. I am indebted to the *New Georgia Encyclopedia* (www.georgiaencyclopedia.org) for permission to quote information related to the religious denominations present in Georgia before 1865. I am also grateful to the South Georgia Conference of the United Methodist Church for permission to include data from their publication *History of the South Georgia Conference (of the) United Methodist Church.* I continue to be indebted to the kindness of postal workers, law enforcement personnel, shop keepers and ordinary citizens who were so helpful in steering me in the right direction to a number of church buildings that were difficult to locate.

Where it seemed appropriate I have included sections from *Antebellum Churches in Georgia* that no doubt readers of my first book will recognize. I believe it is just as important to describe for new readers some of the enormous hardships our forefathers endured while they labored to establish the Christian faith in this sparsely settled land.

We owe a profound debt of gratitude to those hardy pioneers who were our forefathers. They struggled mightily in the vast untamed wilderness to build shelters for their families, clear the timber, till the virgin land, and all the while remaining vigilant so as protect themselves and their neighbors from determined foes. Yet they would often take the time to gather tools in hand, whenever a neighbor needed a new barn or the community needed a new church. These hardy, robust farmers and tradesmen left us a legacy of unselfish devotion and simple faith that endures to this day in these old houses of worship. It is in their memory that *Faith of our Fathers* is respectfully dedicated.

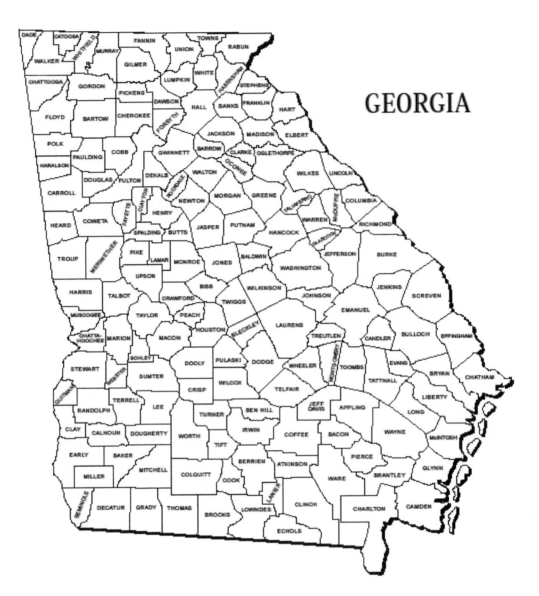

GEORGIA

Carl Vinson Institute of Government
The University of Georgia

6

HISTORICAL MARKERS IN THE STATE OF GEORGIA

(Excerpted from *Antebellum Churches in Georgia)*

Historic markers are found in all sorts of shapes and sizes. Some are metal plaques affixed to walls; some are inscribed stone or marble slabs while others are metal with cast lettering generally on both sides that are mounted on metal posts.

Beginning in the 1930's the federal government undertook the task of erecting metal markers at historically significant sites in each state. This effort was funded under the Works Progress Administration (WPA) primarily to provide jobs during the Great Depression. Few of these WPA markers have survived into our era.

In Georgia, the earliest statewide effort for the preservation of historically noteworthy sites began with the creation of the Georgia Historical Commission by the Georgia Legislature in 1951

The commission enthusiastically embraced its mission and by the mid 1960's had erected almost two thousand markers at various sites throughout the state. These markers were of a uniform size and height and were made of cast aluminum, painted olive green with raised letters painted gold with the same message on both sides. The state seal was centered at the top of the marker and the bottom contained the Georgia Historical Commission's name, the monument number and the date the monument was erected.

By 1968 the commission concluded it had completed its task and that virtually every historically significant site had been identified and appropriately marked. It was also noted that the cost for erecting these markers had escalated from around one hundred twenty dollars in the 1950's to an estimated twelve hundred dollars in 1968.

In the Executive Reorganization Act of 1972 the Georgia Historical Commission was dissolved and its functions were transferred to the newly established Georgia Department of Natural Resources. The DNR designated the State Parks and Historic Sites Division as the responsible state agency to erect new markers and maintain the existing ones. The markers erected or replaced by this agency were almost identical to the older markers except the Georgia Historical Commission name at the bottom of the marker was replaced with the words "Georgia Historical Marker."

In an attempt to privatize certain state functions in the 1990's, the responsibility for maintenance and replacement of historical markers was contracted to a firm located outside the state, but this effort was unsatisfactory and was abandoned after several years.

By 1997 the State of Georgia had discontinued erecting new historical markers although the Department of Natural Resources still retained the responsibility to maintain and replace them as necessary. As more and more markers needed to be repaired or replaced, the background color of many ranged from dark green to brown. That same year the Georgia General Assembly transferred the responsibility for erecting new historical markers to the Georgia Historical Society, a private, non-profit organization chartered by the State of Georgia in 1839. The Georgia

Historical Society also assumed responsibility for considering and approving applications for new historical markers.

The new markers erected by the Georgia Historical Society are the same size, shape and material as the older markers, but differ in that they are painted black and have white painted raised letters and the Georgia Historical Society seal replaces the State of Georgia seal at the top center of the marker. Sponsor's names accompany the Society's at the bottom of each marker.

To qualify for a marker, buildings, structures and sites for special events typically must be at least 50 years old. Nominations concerning individuals generally require the subject to have been deceased at least 25 years. All nominations must be sponsored by at least one entity such as a church, historical organization, school, government or corporation. The Society's marker program is set up on a matching basis with the sponsor agreeing to pay fifty percent of the direct cost of casting and delivering the marker. In 2006 the average total cost was $2,500. The sponsor also accepts the responsibility for maintenance of the marker.

In addition to official state markers erected by the Georgia Historical Commission, Department of Natural Resources and the Georgia Historical Society, numerous other organizations within the state have been involved in erecting new markers, most notably the Historic Chattahoochee Commission, the Daughters of the American Revolution, Colonial Dames of Georgia, Sons of Confederate Veterans, United Daughters of the Confederacy, various armed forces veterans organizations, churches, colleges and schools, counties and cities, garden clubs, county historical societies and the Atlantic Coastal Highway Commission.

Some of these markers are similar in materials, size and shape to official state markers while others are entirely different. Where any of these markers are present at church sites included here, the contents of these markers are included in whole or in part and are credited to the appropriate organization. Please note that when the wording of any historical marker is cited, no effort has been made to change the original spelling, punctuation or grammatical construction.

Organizations, State Agencies or Other Entities that have erected markers in Georgia are often recognized by the abbreviations listed below which will be utilized in this book:

GHC	Georgia Historical Commission
GHS	Georgia Historical Society
GHM	Georgia Historical Marker (GA. Dept. of Nat. Resources)
HCC	Historic Chattahoochee Commission
WPA	United States Work Progress Administration
ACH	Atlantic Coastal Highway Commission
GCG	Garden Clubs of Georgia
GSCD	Georgia Society of Colonial Dames
SCV	Sons of Confederate Veterans
DAR	Daughters of the American Revolution
UDC	United Daughters of the Confederacy
GTHP	Georgia Trust for Historic Preservation

EARLY CHRISTIAN FOOTPRINTS IN GEORGIA

(Excerpted from *Antebellum Churches in Georgia*)

Within the last two decades, archeological research has provided exciting evidence that the Christian faith in Georgia had its beginning more than four hundred and fifty years ago. Some historians maintain that Georgia was the setting for the first European effort to establish a colony in what has since become the United States of America.

There is evidence that Lucas Vasquez Ayllon, a Spanish explorer and adventurer who was the discoverer of the Chesapeake Bay, founded the colony of San Miguel de Gualdupe in the area of the Sapelo Sound (McIntosh County) in 1526, less than thirty four years after Christopher Columbus first sighted the New World.

Forty years later, in 1566, Pedro Menendez de Aviles, who had founded the Spanish colony of St. Augustine in Florida the year before, had begun to establish a series of missions on the barrier islands between St. Augustine and the Savannah River. These missions, staffed at first by Jesuit priests and later by Franciscan friars, ministered to the Guale Indians. By 1570 a mission called Santa Cataline de Guale had been established on what is now St. Catherine's Island. Other early Spanish missions in the area included San Jose de Sapala on Sapelo Island, Santa Domingo de Asao and San Simon on St. Simon's Island and San Pedro de Mocama on Cumberland Island. The Guale Indians who had at first welcomed the Spanish missionaries revolted in 1597 against what they considered Spanish oppression and five Franciscan priests were tragically killed during the ensuing frontier conflict. For a brief time the missions were abandoned, but by 1603 the fighting was over and the Franciscan missionaries returned to the missions. For the next half-century the Spanish missions enjoyed relatively peaceful relations with the Indians. But then the English established Charleston as the capitol of their South Carolina colony in 1670, an action that was seen as a direct threat by the Spanish to their territorial claims. After a series of sharp border clashes with the English over the next sixteen years, Spanish authorities reluctantly decided to abandon all missions north of the St. Mary's River. Santa Cataline de Guale was abandoned by 1680.

Because Spain had not relinquished its claim to the area in which the abandoned missions lay and concerned with French territorial ambitions that might imperil their South Carolina colony, the English government sought to establish frontier forts in the disputed area, but these efforts ultimately failed because of the primitive living conditions and low morale of the soldiers in the vast wilderness.

As the English government pondered ways and means of protecting its South Carolina colony, a young soldier recently back from European wars was elected to Parliament and was about to capture the imagination of the British public. James Edward Oglethorpe was named to chair a parliamentary committee the task of which was to investigate the conditions to be found in English prisons of the day. Finding these conditions so abysmal, Oglethorpe wrote a scathing report condemning many existing policies governing incarceration. Perhaps the worst abuses were those which caused a citizen to be jailed indefinitely simply for falling into debt. After the report became public, Oglethorpe became a figure of national prominence. He began to consider ways to moderate prison sentences, especially for those imprisoned for debt and conceived the idea that debtors could be rehabilitated if given the opportunity to start fresh in a new country.

The prospect of establishing a new colony excited the imagination of a number of English gentlemen who were interested in pursuing their own causes and wealth enhancing possibilities in the New World. Soon they joined together forming a board of twenty-one members under Oglethorpe's leadership and in 1730 they petitioned King George for a royal charter permitting them to found a new colony to be located between the Savannah and Altamaha rivers. The colony was to be called "Georgia" in honor of the king. Within two years the charter was granted and the group was incorporated as 'Trustees for Establishing the Colony of Georgia in America' with authority to legislate for its government over a period of twenty-one years. After the twenty-one years, the grant was to return to the king.

As a result of intense discussion within the group and no doubt much input from the royal court, the Trustees apparently settled on four major goals for their enterprise.

- First they would endeavor to create a place where "the worthy poor" could rehabilitate themselves through rigorous manual labor.
- Second they believed the new colony could produce "exotic" plants and products, which England was at that time forced to import from foreign lands.
- Third, and most important to the English government, the new colony would serve as an armed buffer between their settlers in South Carolina and the Spanish in Florida.
- Fourth, the Trustees had a sincere desire to provide a place of refuge for the persecuted Protestants in Europe.

Concerning religion, the Trustees made it clear that the colonists were free to worship God as they saw fit. With the exception of Catholics and Jews, all colonists were accorded the free exercise of religion as long as this exercise caused no offense or scandal to the government.

After careful selection by the Trustees, in November 1732, some 114 men, women and children accompanied by Oglethorpe, who the trustees designated as leader, set sail on the ship *Anne* for a two-month journey across the Atlantic to Charleston. After a brief rest there, they traveled to Port Royal, South Carolina's most southern settlement. Oglethorpe with South Carolina governor Col. William Bull and some South Carolina militia went ahead of them and traveled seventeen miles up the Savannah River. There, on Yamacraw Bluff, high above the southern bank of the river, Oglethorpe found an ideal location to establish the new settlement and that settlement became what is now Savannah. In 1733, a Church of England congregation was organized there.

The English government considered the new territory to be merely an extension of the South Carolina colony, but the Spanish looked at this new settlement with growing alarm. To them it was seen as a direct challenge to their Florida colony and a formidable obstacle to their designs on South Carolina. To the French it seemed to be clear evidence that England intended to move westward, threatening to sever communications between Canada and the Louisiana settlements.

For more than a decade after 1732 hostilities between the English, the French and the Spanish dominated the southern colonies in North America.

Two years after founding Savannah, Oglethorpe returned to England where he gathered a second group of settlers for the new colony. This group included both John and Charles Wesley and twenty-six German Moravians seeking to escape religious persecution in Europe. Within two years of its founding, the new settlement at Savannah included Presbyterians from Scotland and Lutherans, Saltzburgers and other German Protestants all of whom established their denominations within the settlement. Even English Jews, who were officially banned from the colony, organized a synagogue there in 1733. It is claimed that John Wesley studied German so that he could communicate with Jewish settlers in Georgia.

During the first years of the colony's existence during a health crisis, Oglethorpe greeted an arriving ship carrying some forty-three Jews including a medical doctor, Dr. Samuel Nunes. At the time, Jews were not acceptable as colonists, but the colony needed a doctor as well as settlers so the Jewish passengers were allowed to remain.

While Oglethorpe spent the first few years building fortifications around Savannah and in other areas south of the new town including Frederica on St. Simon's Island, the Spanish also prepared for war. The conflict, which erupted in 1739, was in large measure a result of disputed commerce along America's southern coastal regions and in the Caribbean. Spain was determined to expel the English from the territory both nations claimed. But Oglethorpe moved first, sending an invasion force of British and Indians to mount a siege against the Spanish at St. Augustine in Florida. Oglethorpe's force was defeated north of St. Augustine so the siege was abandoned and the English hurried back to St. Simon's Island to prepare for the inevitable Spanish military counter attack.

In 1742 a Spanish invasion force of fifty ships appeared off St. Simons and landed over three thousand Spanish troops. A combined force of British regulars from Fort Frederica and Scotch Highlanders from nearby Darien surprised the Spanish at Bloody Marsh and defeated them. The Spanish commander, fearing what he mistakenly believed to be superior forces, ordered a retreat and the Spanish sailed back to St. Augustine. The English colony was never again threatened and a peace treaty between the English and Spanish was signed in 1748.

After the Battle of Bloody Marsh, Oglethorpe again invaded Florida and made a second unsuccessful attack on St. Augustine in 1743. That same year he sailed for England to face charges brought against him by a military subordinate. Though he was cleared of all charges, he never again returned to Georgia. In later years, he was active in support of the independence movement in the American colonies and he lived long enough to see the birth of the United States of America.

Peace with Spain meant the colony of Georgia was no longer the focal point of English interest in America and the Trustees no longer had the need for a large military presence. The colonists who remained turned their attention to acquiring additional land for agricultural development. Many others, however, abandoned their holdings to seek land in Carolina and to acquire slaves which had been forbidden by the Trustees in the Georgia colony. By 1743, fewer than three hundred colonists remained in Savannah. When the British military was disbanded in 1749, there were fewer than one hundred fifty colonists left in Frederica. Coupled with the loss of settlers, the decline and eventual loss of financial support from Parliament and flagging interest in the affairs of the colony by many of its members, the Trustees surrendered their charter to the king in 1752.

By 1758 the Church of England became the established church of the colony. The Commons House of Assembly that same year created eight parishes which were separate administrative entities accountable to the Assembly and to the royal governor. Four more parishes were created later. Local landowners who were members of the Church of England usually elected the officials for each parish. After the American Revolution, these parishes became known as counties and are political subdivisions of Georgia today.

The colony of Georgia was divided into parishes to facilitate the establishment of Church of England congregations, but despite favoring them, the English government nevertheless was quietly supportive of other Protestant denominations perhaps to encourage rapid population growth in the new "buffer" colony. The crown and the Colonial Assembly seemed to tolerate most Dissenters and were generally responsive to petitions requesting land on which to build denominational churches. The colony consisted of Presbyterians, Methodists, Lutherans, Moravians, and Quakers. Roman Catholics were prohibited primarily because the authorities feared they might report intelligence information to the Spanish in Florida.

Many of the colonists were dissatisfied with the rules prohibiting slavery and alcohol in Georgia. They petitioned the Trustees and slavery became legal in 1749 despite the opposition of those who had emigrated for religious reasons. By 1776 the population in Georgia had grown to around 45,000 individuals, half of them being slaves. There were some large plantations, but most settlers were small farmers. At the time of the American Revolution, the colonists were of divided sentiment.

By 1772 the Baptists established a congregation in Savannah and by 1790 when the colony had become the State of Georgia, Catholics from Maryland were encouraged to establish a church in Savannah.

No history of Christian worship in Georgia would be complete without mentioning the term 'brush arbor.' This is a fitting description for the crude shelters our ancestors built to accommodate religious services in the early years. Sturdy logs formed the corners of these primitive facilities. Long poles were then cut and fastened together to serve as support for a roof comprised of tree branches or hay to shelter the worshippers from the hot summer sun or the cold rains of winter. Rough log benches were placed in parallel rows to seat those attending services while the minister preached from a raised stump.

Most areas of Georgia in these early days were too sparsely settled and too poor to attract full-time ministers. Itinerant ministers or circuit riders would send advance notice of their plans to visit a community by a certain date so that arbors could be renovated or constructed and the widely scattered rural families could gather and take part in the services. These services would last for a few days or sometimes for several weeks. Most of the time, spiritual enthusiasm in the 'brush arbors' ran high and many participants were recorded as having 'found religion' in these primitive shelters.

As more and more settlers moved into these rural areas, the need for more adequate church facilities became apparent. The next development was the gathering of volunteers in the community to erect or 'raise up' the walls of a more permanent house of worship. This process was often referred to as a 'church raising.' Once the decision had been made to 'raise a church', word was sent to rural households setting the date for construction to begin. On that date, dozens of volunteers gathered, cut the timber and raised a rough log building, often in the space of a single day. These log churches were some of the first permanent buildings in these settlements.

Within a few years the community outgrew these rough log facilities and, with the advent of the saw mill, the construction of much larger and more attractive frame church facilities became feasible. Since it frequently took a week or more to cut the timber, saw the lumber and erect these new houses of worship, the families of the volunteer builders would gather to prepare meals for the workers. These occasions provided rare opportunities for social interaction, hymn singing, bible lessons and preaching.

Most of these rural structures were simple, one story frame rectangular buildings containing one large room. It was quite common for these structures to have two front entrance doors, one for the males and one for the females. In the larger churches one would often find a raised gallery designed to accommodate slaves. The more prosperous cities and towns frequently erected masonry church facilities which were designed by prominent American architects and constructed by professional builders. Because these were usually built with brick or stone rather than wood, a number have survived relatively untouched by exterior renovation.

GEORGIA: THE FIRST 130 YEARS

Three churches featured in this book were constructed before the American Revolution. All the others included in this book were completed before 1865, the final year of the Civil War. The oldest church in this book was built less than twenty years after the colony of Georgia was founded. Between 1733 and 1865, much of Georgia's history unfolded.

Great Britain established a total of thirteen colonies in America. Georgia was the most recent since it was founded in 1733 by General Oglethorpe. Less than fifty years later in 1774 the First Continental Congress met in Philadelphia to consider what action should be taken to address the grievances the colonists felt had been committed by Great Britain. Twelve of the thirteen colonies sent delegates; Georgia declined. At that moment in time, despite growing anti-British feelings, Georgia was threatened with attacks by the Creek Indians and it needed the active support of the British army to combat this threat. In addition the royal governor, Sir James Wright, was particularly effective in addressing the colonists' most egregious concerns.

Meanwhile in Philadelphia the First Continental Congress submitted a statement of their concerns to the British crown and adjourned after agreeing to meet in the spring of the next year should the crown ignore or dismiss their concerns. The months that followed witnessed the shedding of blood in skirmishes between British soldiers and colonists in New England at Lexington and Concord. Accordingly, the Second Continental Congress was convened in May of 1775 and this time delegates from Georgia were sent although they did not arrive until that fall. These representatives were instructed to offer a pledge of Georgia's full support for the defense of the colonies.

On July 4, 1776, the Declaration of Independence was ratified by the Second Continental Congress and signed by the three Georgia representatives, Button Gwinnett, Lyman Hall and George Walton. Every representative who signed this document did so in full knowledge that if the war with England was lost, they were subject to be executed for treason.

During the next two years Georgia escaped much of the fighting going on to the north. By December of 1778, however, Savannah was attacked and overwhelmed by a British force that went on to besiege Augusta. That same year the British burned Midway Congregational Church. Georgia could do little to defend itself. Its militia was too small and poorly armed. Soon the British army took control and Royal Governor Wright returned to Savannah. It was during this period that the British used Jerusalem Lutheran Church as a hospital and stable. Although colonists continued the fight, the British remained firmly in control of Georgia. It was not until June of 1781 that the Georgia militia and units of the Continental army were able to drive the British out of Augusta. The following spring the British evacuated Savannah and in September of 1783 representatives of Great Britain, France and the American states signed the Treaty of Paris which granted independence to the former thirteen colonies. Two years later General Oglethorpe died at the age of eighty eight. The man who had founded the colony had lived long enough to see it win independence from England and become an integral part of the United States of America.

Land became the chief issue in Georgia after the Revolutionary War. The state was rich in land, but was poor in other resources. Land that had belonged to the Tories, those colonists who had remained loyal to the British crown, was confiscated and made available to Georgians and others who had fought for independence. The Indian tribes were forced to cede more and more of their ancestral lands which were taken over by white settlers. Although the inhabitants of Georgia were for the most part small scale farmers and tradespeople, the invention of the cotton gin made it feasible to cultivate cotton and many large tracts of land were assembled by planters who needed slave labor in order to profitably bring cotton to the market.

In the 1790 census Georgia had 82,548 people. Ten years later the population had grown to 162,686. By 1840 the state had 691,000 people. In 1860 just before the outbreak of hostilities in the Civil War, Georgia had a population of just over one million inhabitants, including 593,000 whites and 466,000 blacks. The state was still primarily rural in character and it has been estimated that just six percent of the white population owned almost half of Georgia's property. Three fourths of the white male population was engaged in agriculture on farms that averaged around one hundred acres or less. By the end of 1860 the state had produced and exported 702,000 bales of cotton to feed the hungry mills of the North and Europe.

In addition to their labor in the cotton fields, planters tended to hire out their slaves on annual contracts to work on building the rapidly expanding railroad system or in other industrial enterprises.

After many years of caustic debate over the subject of slavery, states of the Deep South where cotton was king warily watched the presidential election of 1860. They were convinced that the election of Abraham Lincoln would mean that the whole issue of cotton production, by far their major source of wealth, would be put in jeopardy. These states had gone on record to say that the election of Lincoln would cause them to secede from the federal union. In January of 1861 in a special convention at the state capitol in Milledgeville a secession ordinance was proposed to the 297 delegates. It passed with 208 votes. By February of that year, South Carolina, Georgia, Florida, Alabama, Louisiana, Mississippi and Texas had joined to become the Confederate States of America. A little later Virginia, Arkansas, Tennessee and North Carolina seceded from the union and joined the Confederacy.

Four years of war brought great suffering to the people of Georgia. Federal forces succeeded early on in blockading southern ports including Savannah and Darien effectively shutting down the export of cotton and lumber to European markets and the import of finished goods from Europe to the state. Most of the eligible young men had enlisted in the Confederate army and were away campaigning with Gen. Robert E. Lee in Virginia. After the Confederate victory over the Union army at Chickamauga in North Georgia in 1863, the tide of war turned against the South when Gen. William T. Sherman and his 112,000 man Union army crossed into Georgia from Tennessee to confront the 60,000 Confederates under Gen. Joseph E. Johnston in the spring of 1864. In a series of bloody battles from Dalton to Resaca to Kennesaw Mountain and finally to the outskirts of Atlanta in July of 1864 both sides fought valiantly, but the Confederates were forced to retreat into the fortifications in the city. Then, with Gen. Johnston being replaced by Gen. John Bell Hood, the Confederates launched a series of counter attacks against the much larger Union forces with disastrous consequences for the Southern army. Although Union forces lost around four thousand as casualties, the Confederate losses were twice that high. Gen. Hood was forced to burn his supplies and evacuate Atlanta. Seeking to draw Gen. Sherman northward, Hood marched toward Tennessee, but Sherman refused to follow and instead began his march south toward Savannah against only token resistance. Leaving a path of utter destruction in his wake, Gen. Sherman captured Savannah in December, 1864, effectively severing the lower South from the Confederacy. By April of 1865, the war was over and Georgia lay in ruins.

RELIGIOUS DENOMINATIONS IN GEORGIA
1733 – 1865

Virtually all recognized Christian religious groups are present in Georgia at the present time. Since the focus of this book is limited to the oldest still standing churches in this state, the denominations included here represent only those religious groups that were present circa 1732 - 1865. The denominational information presented here is excerpted by permission from *The New Georgia Encyclopedia* (w.w.w.georgiaencyclopedia.com)

Anglican Church

The impact of the Anglican Church, or Church of England, in Georgia reaches beyond religion, for it was largely due to the political influence of the church's key members that the English established the colony of Georgia in 1733. Before the American Revolution (1775-1783).

Anglicans constituted the largest and most influential group of Christians in Georgia.

Anglicanism originated in the sixteenth century, when Henry VIII left the Roman Catholic Church to establish the new state church. At the time Georgia was founded, anyone holding a political position in England was required to be Anglican.

James Edward Oglethorpe, the founder of the Georgia colony, was a member of the British Parliament in the 1720s, before he ventured to America. With the new colony, Oglethorpe sought a more humanitarian way for England to deal with its "worthy poor," who at the time were often incarcerated for indebtedness. Other members of Parliament hoped to convert Native Americans in the region to Christianity, while the British government saw a need to for a political and military buffer to protect its colonies in Virginia and the Carolinas against possible encroachment by the Spanish, who had colonized Florida. Sending settlers to Georgia promised a way to meet all three of these needs. Missionary priests (Anglican ministers) would provide moral leadership to the colonists and preach to the Native Americans, while the settlements established by these newcomers would act as a barrier against Spanish incursion.

Among those working with Oglethorpe was the influential Anglican priest Thomas Bray, founder of the Society for the Propagation of the Gospel to Foreign Parts. Bray had for thirty years worked with other church members to send missionaries to English colonies. One major thrust of (Bray's) activities was the solicitation of donations to pay missionaries' salaries. Another was the provision of books for the missionaries. Bray's group sent books by the caseload, intending them to be used by the ministers and to form "a publick library" in the new colony.

Although there was some discussion of the establishment of the Church of England as the official church of Georgia, groups of various persuasions were permitted to worship in the new colony. The Trustees did appoint Anglican clergymen to serve the new colonists, however, and saw to it that 300 acres were provided for the support of an Anglican church in Savannah, including a parsonage and cemetery.

The first priest selected by the Trustees was a volunteer, Henry Herbert, who sailed with the original colonists, reaching Georgia in 1733. Herbert founded Christ Church of Savannah, the first Anglican parish, or self-supporting congregation, in Georgia; but he died during his return voyage to England before the year ended. The trustees appointed a series of nine Anglican priests in the first twelve years of the colony.

The Trustees also established charity schools to ensure that children understood the Anglican catechism. Teachers were supervised by Anglican clergymen, but children of all faiths were invited to attend. (Indians; Sephardic, or Spanish-speaking Jews; Huguenots; and Moravians were among those living in the environs. One of the prime results of those charity schools was the ready acceptance of English as the official language.

Perhaps the best-known Anglican priest in Georgia's history is John Wesley, appointed by the Trustees to serve as rector, or the priest in charge of a parish, of Savannah's Christ Church in 1735. John Wesley's brother, Charles Wesley, served as resident minister of Frederica for a brief time in the 1730s, and by 1751 Augusta and Savannah each had an Anglican clergyman in residence.

Unwilling to leave the faith when the colonists revolted, Anglicans in America formally reconstituted themselves in 1789 as the Protestant Episcopal Church in the United States of America. Other than political affiliations, the tenets of the faith were not changed, and Anglicans in America are generally known as Episcopalians.

Baptist Church

One or two Baptists arrived in Savannah with James Oglethorpe, and others soon followed. Tiny Baptist centers were formed in the Savannah and Augusta areas. The first Baptist church, Tuckaseeking Seventh-Day (in Effingham County), existed from 1759 to about 1763. In 1772 the first continuing Baptist church, Kiokee, was founded near Appling; twelve years later the first continuing Baptist association in the state, the Georgia Association, appeared with a membership of five churches in two counties. Thereafter other churches and associations were constituted as the population spread throughout the state.

After several failed attempts at union early in the nineteenth century, in 1822 the largest group of Baptists formed a general body that gradually encompassed churches statewide. Today (this body is) called the Georgia Baptist Convention.

Other Baptist church organizations include:

First African Baptist Church – With the coming of freedom, the Zion Baptist Association (founded in the Savannah area in 1865) was the first African American general body in the state; it was followed, over the years, by about 200 other associations.

Independent Baptists – (Some) Baptists in Georgia have chosen not to participate in any association and/or convention. Shortly after the Georgia Baptist Convention was initiated, some churches and associations identified themselves as missionary but opted to remain independent from the convention. Many independent churches are located in rural areas and favor temperance, foot washing, ministers without theological training, and associational missions. Their primary focus is on worship, mutual encouragement, and localized benevolences.

Free Will Baptists – Free Will Baptists are an Arminian Baptist denomination with origins in the seventeenth and eighteenth centuries. Followers of the doctrine of the Dutch theologian Jacobus Arminius, they reject the Calvinist belief in absolute predestination, maintaining instead that salvation is open to all.

Primitive Baptists – Primitive Baptists emerged as a distinct denomination during the early nineteenth century in response to the growing importance of missionary efforts in the Baptist church. The Primitive Baptists opposed such efforts, embracing a more conservative theology that relied upon such established ideas and traditions of the Calvinist doctrine of predestination and a literal interpretation of the Bible.

African American Baptists – Baptists have been the largest African American religious group in Georgia since the late eighteenth century. Baptist churches have made vital contributions to the identity of black people in the state by shaping behavior and belief, serving as centers of community life, and creating independent spaces free from the control of white society.

Traveling preachers first brought the Baptist message into Georgia during the American Revolution (1775-1783). Baptists (along with Methodists) proclaimed an intensely individualistic, emotional Christian message that called for a decisive, unambiguous conversion experience as the hallmark of a genuine Christian life. The evangelical message found a receptive audience among a wide variety of hearers, including slaves and free blacks in the Georgia colony.

Catholic Church

The Catholic Church in Georgia is both one of the earliest and one of the fastest-growing religious institutions in the state. Today approximately 425,000 Catholics reside in Georgia and are served by either the Archdiocese of Atlanta or the Diocese of Savannah. The Catholic Church established itself in Georgia long before James Oglethorpe founded the colony.

Spanish priests came to Georgia in the sixteenth and seventeenth centuries to convert Native Americans. The Spanish missions had limited success. Although the Jesuit and Franciscan orders managed to win over some locals, Catholicism failed to persevere once the British arrived. Oglethorpe led the British effort to establish a colony in Georgia. He hoped to create an enlightened society in Britain's southernmost American colony, while the British wanted Georgia to serve as a buffer zone between (Protestant) British Carolina to the north and (Catholic) Spanish Florida to the south. In recognition of its role as a military buffer and a haven for religious outcasts, however, the colony forbade the practice of Catholicism. Catholics would not find acceptance in Georgia until the American Revolution (1775-1783).

Christian Church

The Christian Church (Disciples of Christ) is a Protestant group that has been active in Georgia since the early nineteenth century. As its name suggests, the church is the result of the union between two separate Protestant groups. In 1803 Presbyterian minister Barton Stone (1772-1844) formed a religious body known as "Christians" in Kentucky after a Presbyterian synod censured him for ministering to non-Presbyterians. Another Presbyterian clergyman, Thomas Campbell

(1763-1854), began his "Disciples of Christ" group in southwest Pennsylvania in 1807 because of a similar religious censure. Both leaders shared similar beliefs, especially an emphasis on church unity.

Their geographical proximity and theological affinities led Stone and Campbell to unite their congregations in 1832. This union resulted in the current Christian Church (Disciples of Christ), also known as the Stone-Campbell movement.

Congregational Church

American Congregationalism is a direct descendant of sixteenth and seventeenth century Puritanism, which began as a protest movement in England's national Anglican Church. Congregational churches have been active in Georgia since the eighteenth century.

Puritanism was founded on, among other things, a belief in God's supreme authority as expressed in the Bible, simplicity of worship, and opposition to the supremacy of a monarch in the church. Congregational Puritans emphasized representative church government and often took the form of separatist groups that fully repudiated the Church of England.

The major source of American Congregationalism, however, resulted from a group of English and Dutch nonseparatist Congregationalists who sailed to America in 1620 to escape religious persecution in their home countries. Known as Pilgrims, the Congregationalists founded a colony at Plymouth, in present day Massachusetts, and paved the way for others to follow. In 1630 a group of Congregationalists, largely from England's Devon, Dorset, and Somersetshire counties, landed at Plymouth and subsequently founded the colony of Dorchester in Massachusetts. These were the ancestors of immigrants who later formed the Midway settlement in Georgia, thirty miles south of Savannah.

Midway Congregational Church played a significant role in the early history of Colonial Georgia. While the still-young colony was hesitant to support the revolutionary cause, the Georgia Puritans independently took part in the Second Continental Congress by sending Lyman Hall, a Midway resident, to represent them. Hall and Button Gwinnett, also from Midway, were two of the three Georgia signers of the Declaration of Independence.

Lutheran Church

Lutheranism, with more than 60 million members, is the largest of the Protestant denominations. It was founded in the early sixteenth century when a German monk, Martin Luther, protested the Roman Catholic Church's practice of selling indulgencies as part of the penance, or punishment, for those who sinned against church teachings. Lutheranism is thus central to the Protestant Reformation and, aided by the rulers of many German principalities rebelling against the centralized power of the Holy Roman Empire, it rapidly spread throughout Germany and Scandinavia. It was imported into the Georgia colony in the early eighteenth century and by the turn of the millennium had established itself as a significant denomination within the state.

Under the direction of German baron Philip Georg Frederick von Reck, a group of forty-six Lutherans arrived in Georgia in 1734, a year after James Oglethorpe founded the colony. Mostly religious expatriates from Salzburg, the group eventually settled in 1736 at a site they named New Ebenezer, located twenty miles northwest of Savannah.

Methodist Church

Georgia's deep roots in Methodism reach back to the founders of the Methodist movement. Methodism is a major Protestant community in the state, and it includes four historically related denominations (listed in order of size): the United Methodist Church, the African Methodist Episcopal Church (AME Church), the Christian Methodist Episcopal Church (CME), and the African Methodist Episcopal Church, Zion (AME Zion). These four denominations form the Pan-Methodist Commission on Union, created in 1996, and all share the theological beliefs and organizational structure common to Methodists worldwide.

Scriptures form the primary basis of Methodist theology and doctrine, which are also strongly influenced by the Nicene Creed of the fourth-century Christian church and the Anglican Church's Book of Common Prayer.

In 1735 the Wesley brothers (John and Charles) and (John) Whitefield sailed to the colony of Georgia, where they served in various capacities. Charles Wesley served as secretary to James Edward Oglethorpe and as chaplain at Fort Frederica on St. Simons Island, while John Wesley served as Anglican rector to the colony. Whitefield was an itinerant evangelist.

Presbyterian Church

The Presbyterian Church (U.S.A.) is the largest Presbyterian body in Georgia, with more than 300 congregations and more than 81,000 members as of 2003. The church is also one of the oldest in the state, dating back to the colonial era.

The form of church government provides the name for the Presbyterian Church. The word presbyter (from the Greek presbutereos) means "elder." Presbyterian congregations elect elders to serve on the session, or governing body, of a particular church. The pastor of a congregation serves as the moderator of its session and conducts its meetings. Individual churches in turn are organized into presbyteries, based on geographic area.

Quakers

The Quakers, formally known as the Religious Society of Friends, constitute a small Christian denomination that formed in England in the 1650's in an effort to avoid overly ritualized worship. In 1768 Joseph Maddock, an English Quaker from North Carolina, founded in Georgia the Quaker community of Wrightsboro (named for James Wright, the royal governor of Georgia).

The Quakers, who have a strict policy of nonviolence, initially did not support the Revolutionary War (1775-1783). The Georgia Quakers dismissed from their congregation men who fought in the war but allowed them to rejoin if they apologized. In 1780 and 1781 a group of patriots raided and attacked Wrightsboro; fifty people were killed and buildings were burned.

Because of their antislavery stance, instituted in 1774, the Quakers could no longer compete in the Georgia economy. Gradually, many of them moved to Midwestern states. Of the few who stayed in Wrightsboro (which continued as a town after they left), most renounced their faith.

To be ignorant of what occurred before you were

born is to remain always a child.

Marcus Tullius Cicero

106 BC – 43 BC

THE GREAT AWAKENING

If there was one single event responsible for the religious enthusiasm of our forefathers, it most probably was their eager participation in what was called the Great Awakening. Georgia's long history of participation in the tradition of religious revivalism stems from this undertaking. The Great Awakening was a spiritual revitalization movement that occurred in the American Colonies circa 1740 – 1780. It consisted of a series of revivals conducted by inspired ministers who implanted in the hearts and minds of their people a deep yearning for personal salvation by Jesus Christ rather than an emphasis on organized religious ritual.

Less than a decade after the founding of the colony of Georgia an evangelical Anglican minister from England brought the message of John Wesley's new-found 'Methodism' to the American Colonies. Working from his headquarters in Savannah, George Whitefield brought a novel preaching style to the colonies. Contrary to the preaching method of that day, using no written notes he delivered an extemporaneous message that spoke directly to the hearts of his listeners. Hundreds, even thousands were drawn to his sermons over time, accepted their own sinful estate, and eagerly embraced the salvation of Christ that Whitefield preached.

Because they had never experienced the advantage of state sponsored support, Baptists, Methodists and Presbyterians in Georgia and the other colonists welcomed and adopted Whitefield's revivalist message of personal salvation. The ministers that followed him incorporated his fervent and evangelical preaching style. Methodist circuit riders and Baptist farmer- preachers soon replaced more educated traditional pastors. Unlike their predecessors, these itinerant ministers made a determined effort to preach to everyone including African slaves. As a result of this endeavor very shortly thereafter there was an independent African American church, first in South Carolina and then in Georgia.

The Great Awakening had a dramatic effect on colonial Protestantism. In addition to the thousands who experienced a profound 'conversion,' many others continued membership in more traditional churches, but they no longer remained silent. Some forcefully complained that their ministers were aloof and bound by ritual practices and they worked diligently to change the orientation of their fellow parishioners.

The Great Awakening was not confined to the American Colonies, but swept through the Protestant churches in Europe as well. Today the great Christian evangelical revivals held in large stadiums or auditoriums attract tens of thousands. Television grants even greater access to these revivals. These mega-events are the modern day equivalent of the first revivals conducted during the Great Awakening modeled on the style and content introduced by George Whitefield that profoundly altered the face of Christianity in the American Colonies.

OUR LADY STAR OF THE SEA CATHOLIC CHURCH

Our Lady Star of the Sea Catholic Church is located on Osborne St. in the city of St. Marys, GA. in Camden County.

The chapel building began as a bank in 1840, but the bank failed after seven years. In the early years as a Catholic church many of the parishioners were Acadians who came from Nova Scotia seeking religious freedom. When a new church was constructed in 1958, the chapel was neglected and fell into disrepair. The ladies of the church formed a guild and raised money for the chapel's restoration. Now fully restored it is used for special occasions.

A brass marker attached to the front of the church contains the following inscription:

Our Lady Star of the Sea Catholic Church
C 1847

The sixth parish founded in Georgia. Members bought this former bank building and converted it into their parish church fulfilling the vision of Catholics who had been meeting since early 1800. It served as the parish for over 100 years until a new church was built in 1958 on land deeded to the Catholics by the City of St. Marys. The chapel is still in use and maintained by the parish.

Our Lady Star of the Sea Catholic Church   Circa 1847

ST. MARYS METHODIST CHURCH

St. Marys Methodist Church is located on Conyers St. in the city of St. Marys, GA. in Camden County.

The Methodist Book of Discipline defines Historic Sites as"…buildings, locations, or structures that are specifically related to a significant event, development, or personality in the history of the annual, central, or jurisdictional conference within whose regions the site is located." St. Marys Methodist Church is a designated Methodist Historic Site.

A GHC marker at the site states has the following inscription:

St. Marys Methodist Church
Established 1799-1800
Celebrated Sesqui-Centennial 1949

This church is the oldest religious organization in the city, although not the oldest church building. George Clark served as first missionary to the people in 1792. John Garvin was the first appointed Pastor to St. Marys in 1799. Methodist services were first held in the building erected for a Courthouse.

In 1812 the City of St. Marys deeded the Methodists a lot 200 x 200 ft., still in use at this time. A church built after 1812 was in use until a few years before the War Between the States when the old church was moved to another site and given to the Negro Methodists. The present church was built before the War of 1861-65. While St. Marys was occupied by Federal troops in 1862, this church was used as a Quartermaster's Dept. where animals were butchered.

A new deed was granted this church in 1878. This building was renovated on several occasions. Between 1792-1955, 103 pastors have served this church which was the first charge of Bishop Arthur J. Moore in 1909.

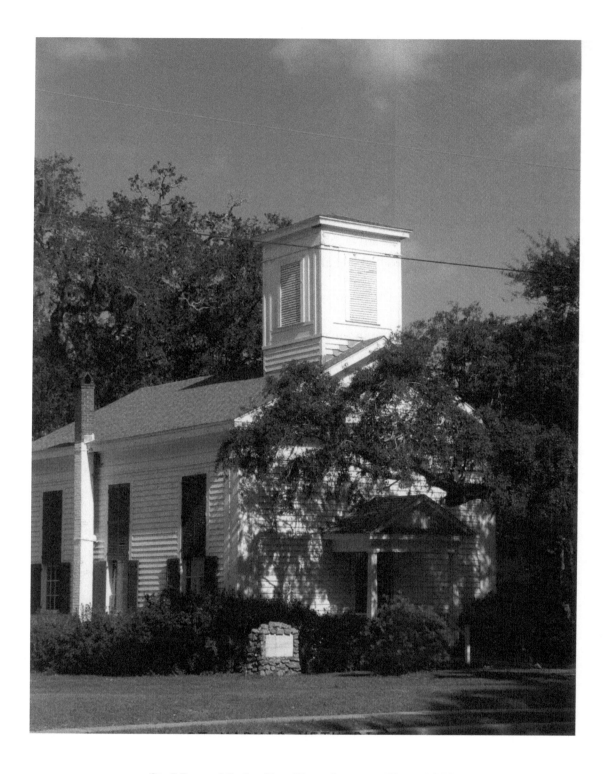

St. Marys Methodist Church   Circa 1855

FIRST PRESBYTERIAN CHURCH OF
ST. MARYS

The First Presbyterian Church is located on Osborne St. at Conyers St. in the city of St. Marys, GA. in Camden County.

A public subscription held on April 2, 1807 resulted in $1,823.50 being raised "…for the promotion of divine worship and for the building of a small but convenient church for that purpose." The completed church was non-denominational until the arrival of the Rev. Pratt from New Brunswick, New Jersey. This church is the oldest Presbyterian Church building in the state of Georgia.

A GHC marker at the site has the following inscription:

First Presbyterian Church

Built by public subscription in 1808, as a place of divine worship for the inhabitants of St. Marys and its vicinity. Reverend Horace Southworth Pratt was ordained and installed as first pastor by the Presbytery of Georgia in June, 1822.

Incorporated under the name of the Independent Presbyterian Church of St. Marys, Dec. 20, 1828. On Dec. 5, 1832, the Independent Church was incorporated as the First Presbyterian Church of St. Marys in the Georgia Presbytery.

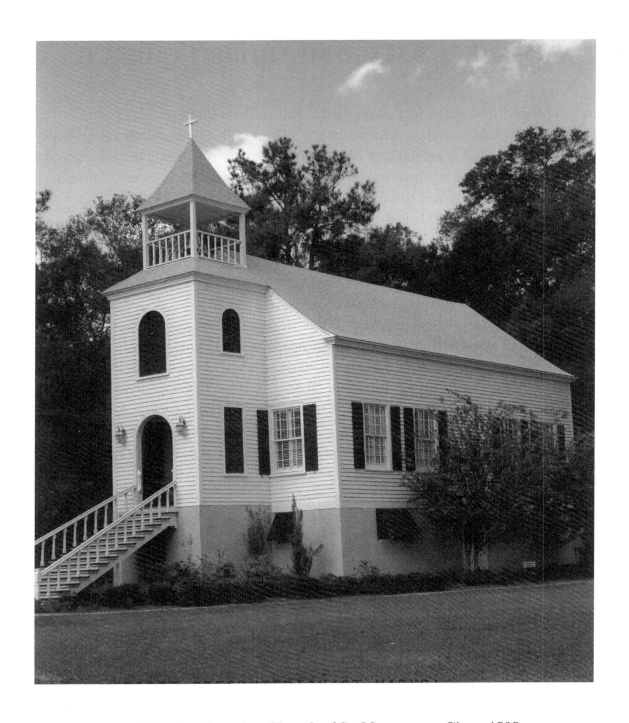

First Presbyterian Church of St. Marys   Circa 1808

EMMANUEL UNITED METHODIST CHURCH

Emmanuel Methodist Church is located on Ratcliff Rd. in Glynn County.

The Methodist Book of Discipline defines Historic Sites as "…buildings, locations, or structures that are specifically related to a significant event, development, or personality in the history of an annual, central, or jurisdictional conference within whose regions the site is located." Emmanuel Methodist Church is a Designated Historical Site.

A South Georgia Conference (Methodist) Church marker at the site has the following inscription:

1800
Emmanuel United Methodist Church

Begun in the year 1800, as New Hope Methodist Church on Laurel Grove Plantation 2 miles S. present site. 1833 original building moved to this site and name changed to Emmanuel. Hand hewn pillars & wooden pegs are visible. 1799 George Clark, sent by Bishop Asbury to St. Mary's, started Methodist Societies in Glynn Co. 1829 Quarterly Conf For St. Mary's and Illa Ct. held here. Wm. Gassoway - pastor; James Helveston - class leader. 1841 St. Illa Ct. (Satilla) became the Brunswick Ct. with Emmanuel as one of the preaching points. Since 1799 Emmanuel has been in continuous service.

Emmanuel Methodist Church   Circa 1833

MIDWAY CONGREGATIONAL CHURCH

Midway Congregational Church is located on U.S. Highway 17 north of U.S. Highway 84 in Liberty County, GA. It was founded in 1754 by a group of English Puritans who migrated from Dorchester, SC. They were given large grants of land to settle there by colonial officials who required a large number of settlers to protect St. John's Parish from the Creek Indians. These first settlers were soon joined by other families from South Carolina, and Great Britain.

The first meeting house was completed in 1756 and the first service was held in 1758. These settlers were Congregationalists in faith and were adamantly in favor of independence from Great Britain and early on favored the American cause. During the Revolutionary War the church and most of the buildings in town were burned by the British. The church was rebuilt in 1792 and has remained essentially untouched by renovation since it was constructed. The walled church cemetery contains about 1200 graves including two Revolutionary War generals and Governor Nathan Brownson. According to Robert Manson in his book, *Children of Pride*, "Perhaps no other spot of equal size encompasses the dust of as many men and women who have shaped the destiny of the state and nation." During the War Between the States, General Sherman's army seized livestock from nearby plantations and kept the animals enclosed in the walled two acre cemetery.

In Colonial times, the Midway settlers worked diligently and developed a strong economy based on agriculture. Rice and indigo were among the chief agricultural products.

A brass marker placed on the front of the church by the DAR has the following inscription:

Midway Congregational Church

Erected 1792. Organized 1754, by descendents of an English Colony which came first to Massachusetts 1630. To Connecticut 1635. To South Carolina 1695. And to Georgia 1752. Built on the same spot as the church which was destroyed by the British in 1778.

This church has given to her country eighty-six ministers of the Gospel and seven foreign missionaries. Midway, in St. John's Parish, now Liberty County, was the cradle of Revolutionary spirit in Georgia and two of her sons were signers of the Declaration of Independence.

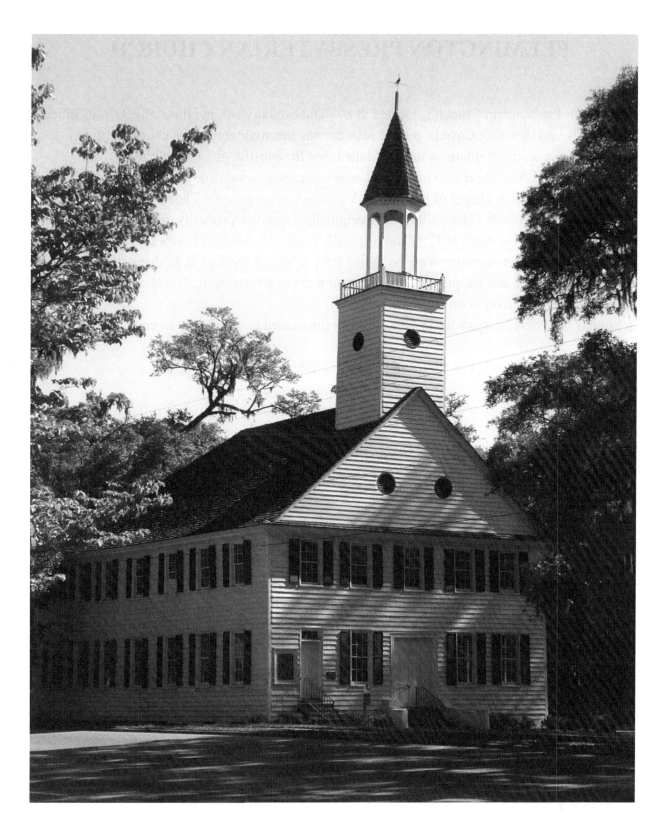

Midway Congregational Church   Circa 1792

FLEMINGTON PRESBYTERIAN CHURCH

Flemington Presbyterian Church is located at 875 Old Sunbury Rd. in Hinesville, GA. in Liberty County. It is said that T.Q. Cassels, a local planter, was the architect for the church. Trained slave carpenters from nearby plantations furnished the labor for constructing the building.

The Church and Society from Gravel Hill was organized some time prior to June 1832. The Church was a branch or chapel of ease of the Midway Congregational Church and was served by ministers of that church. The gallery was originally intended primarily for the slaves of the members. The bell was made in 1799 and originally hung in Midway Church. In 1865 when from force of circumstances members were no longer able to attend services at Midway, they formed a separate organization and adopted the Presbyterian form of government. The church was admitted to the Presbytery of Georgia on April 6, 1865.

A Sunday School was organized in 1836 and has functioned continuously since that time.

A GHC marker at the site has the following inscription:

Flemington Presbyterian Church

Organized in 1815 as the Church and Society of Gravel Hill, this was a branch of Midway Church. The Rev. Robert Quarterman was the first pastor. The first edifice was built in 1836 on land donated by Simon Fraser. This one was completed in 1852. Named Flemington in 1850 honoring William Fleming, it was separated from Midway in 1865. It was admitted to the Georgia Presbytery with the Rev. D.B. Buttolph, pastor; W.E.W. Quarterman, Thomas Cassels, Ezra Stacey, James Laing, elders; S.A. Fraser, L.M. Cassels, deacons. Ezra Stacey was first Sunday School Superintendent. Bell and silver communion service are from Midway Church.

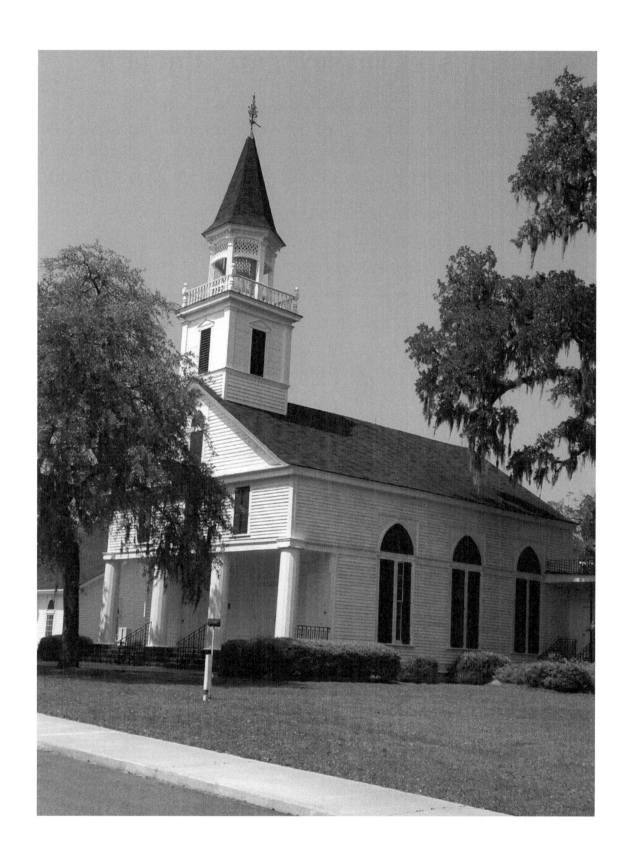

Flemington Presbyterian Church   **Circa 1836**

DORCHESTER PRESBYTERIAN CHURCH

Dorchester Presbyterian Church is located on Brigdon Rd. in Liberty County, GA. approximately one quarter mile south of GA Highway 84. It is said that the church bell that was originally hanging in the church that was burned by the Union forces during the Civil War is now in the bell tower at Dorchester.

A GHC marker at the site has the following inscription:

Dorchester Presbyterian Church

This church, built in 1854 on a lot of four acres donated by B.A. Busbee, was first used for summer services only. On January 6, 1871, it was admitted to the Savannah Presbytery as an organized church of 14 members. The Rev. J.W. Montgomery was the first pastor. L.J. Mallard was the first ruling elder. The bell, from old Sunbury, was once used for church, school, market and town. The font and communion service are from Midway Church. The font was a gift from Dr. William McWhir, the tankard from John Lambent, the communion service from Simon Monroe, Esq. Elders contributing most in later years - Preston Waite and Charles B. Jones.

Dorchester Presbyterian Church   **Circa 1854**

FIRST BAPTIST CHURCH OF SAVANNAH

The First Baptist Church of Savannah is located at 223 Bull St., in Savannah, GA., in Chatham County. It was chartered November 26, 1800 and shortly afterward the first church building was erected on Franklin Square. The cornerstone of the present church was laid February 2, 1831, and the building was completed in 1833. The Greek revival structure is the oldest church in the city. The sanctuary was enlarged in 1839 and was improved at different times and was completely renovated in 1921. Subsequent renovations were made in 1966, 1989-1990, and 1998-1999.

Governor Josiah Tattnall granted the church a perpetual charter on December 19, 1801 addressed to "the Deacons of the Baptist Church in Savannah." The church has been called the First Baptist Church since February 4, 1847. The Sunday school was organized on April 29, 1827. The first pastor, Henry Holcombe, edited the Analytical Repository, reputed to be the earliest religious magazine in the South and the first Baptist missionary magazine in the nation. The second pastor, William Bullein Johnson, became the first president of the Southern Baptist Convention.

Josiah Penfield, a deacon of the church, left a bequest of $2,500 to the Georgia Baptist Convention in 1828 which was the first money utilized to establish what is now Mercer University. This church was among the very few Southern coastal churches to remain open during the Civil War. The week before Savannah surrendered to Gen. Sherman, pastor Sylvanus Landrum preached to a congregation composed largely of Confederate soldiers. The next week, his congregation was made up largely of Union soldiers who occupied the city.

A GHS historical marker at the site has the following inscription:

First Baptist Church

First Baptist Church, Savannah's oldest standing house of worship, was designed by Elias Carter and completed in 1833. The congregation dates to 1800. In 1922 the front of the building was extended, a cupola removed, and the edifice was covered with limestone. Under the leadership of Sylvanus Landrum, First Baptist Church was one of few southern churches to remain open during the Civil War. Notable pastors include W.L. Pickard, later president of Mercer University; Norman Cox, executive secretary of the Historical Commission of the Southern Baptist Convention; and Arthur Jackson, executive secretary of the Georgia Baptist Foundation.

First Baptist Church of Savannah   Circa 1833

TRINITY UNITED METHODIST CHURCH

Trinity United Methodist Church is located at 225 West President St., in Savannah, GA. in Chatham County. The church is located on a lot that was part of the garden of the Telfair family. The congregation paid $8,500 for the lot and raised $20,000 to build the sanctuary which was completed in 1850. The solid masonry walls are constructed of brick and covered with stucco. Native Georgia pine was hand planed for the framing, the flooring and wainscoting.

The architect, John B. Hogg (1826-1880) modeled the building after the Wesley Chapel in London. The mason for the church was Norbonne Radcliffe and the carpenters were John F. Sturtevant and Francis Blair.

A GHC marker at the site bears the following inscription:

Trinity Methodist Church
Mother Church of Savannah Methodism

Trinity Church is the oldest Methodist Church in a city whose intimate association with John Wesley and George Whitfield gives it a unique place in the history of Methodism.

The cornerstone of the building was laid February 14, 1848, in a ceremony presided over by the Reverend Alfred T. Mann, Pastor. The edifice, which was completed in 1850, is in the Corinthian order of architecture and was designed by John B. Hogg of Savannah.

Prior to the erection of Trinity Church the Methodist congregation in Savannah worshipped in Wesley Chapel on South Broad Street. Among the great preachers of the Methodist Church whose names are associated with the Chapel are Francis Asbury, William Capers, John Howard, James C. Andrew, Ignatius Few, Elijah Sinclair and George C. Pierce. Through their faith and service others have lived more valiantly.

Trinity Methodist Church   **Circa 1850**

FIRST AFRICAN BAPTIST CHURCH

The First African Baptist Church is located at 23 Montgomery St., in Savannah, GA., in Chatham County. It is said to be the oldest black church in North America having been founded by Rev. George Leile, who had been born a slave in South Carolina. In 1778, Rev. Leile and some fifty slave members of his congregation fled to Savannah to take refuge with the British during the American Revolutionary War. The church was constituted in December, 1783 and Rev. Leile served as its first pastor.

In 1782, Rev. Leile baptized Andrew Bryan and his wife, Hannah. Bryan was ordained January 20, 1788. When Rev. Leile left Savannah with the British at the conclusion of the American Revolution, Rev. Bryan secured his slave master's permission to become the church's second pastor. In 1794 the congregation erected a frame structure on Bryan St. and the church was named the Bryan Street African Baptist Church. By 1800 the congregation had grown to approximately 700 members. Under Rev. Bryan's leadership, the church continued to prosper and purchased the site upon which the present church building is located.

It is claimed that the first black Sunday school in the nation was formed in the church with the assistance of the Independent Presbyterian Church on July 26, 1826.

Members of the congregation provided the labor for erecting the present church building in 1859. Many were slaves who worked on the building after their daily chores had been completed.

Breathing holes are located in the downstairs floor and are said to have provided air for slaves fleeing to freedom by way of a secret tunnel leading from the church to the Savannah River. Balcony pews still retain the African names of artisans who worked on the building.

The church is listed on the National Register of Historic Places and is considered to be the first brick structure owned by blacks in the State of Georgia.

First African Baptist Church   Circa 1859

UNITARIAN UNIVERSALIST CHURCH

The Unitarian Universalist Church is located at 307 East Harris St., in Savannah, GA., in Chatham County. It was built in 1851 by John Norris and was presented as a gift to the Unitarian congregation in Savannah by Moses Eastman, a New Hampshire silversmith. The church was the first public building in Savannah to be lighted by natural gas. President Millard Fillmore attended a service in this church in 1854.

The church fell victim to the country's sectional disputes, which divided the nation in the period leading up to the Civil War, and closed in 1859 despite the intense efforts of the minister and congregation. It is said only two Unitarian churches in the South, one in Charleston and one in New Orleans, remained active during the Civil War. The organist of this church before it closed in 1859 was James L. Pierpont, the brother of the minister, who gave singing lessons in the church. He also wrote the famous song, "One Horse Open Sleigh" which was copywrited in 1857 and later became known as "Jingle Bells." When his brother, Rev. John Pierpont, returned to Boston at the war's outset, James remained in Savannah, married the mayor's daughter and served in the First Georgia Cavalry.

The congregation of St. Stephen's Episcopal Church, the first African-American Episcopal Church in Georgia, purchased the building. It was moved on rollers to its present location where it served that congregation until 1947. Southern Baptists worshipped in the building until 1997 when the Unitarian Universalists purchased it returning it to its Unitarian roots.

A private marker located across from Troup Square has the following inscription:

"Jingle Bells"

James L. Pierpont (1822-1893), composer of "Jingle Bells", served as music director of this church in the 1850's when it was a Unitarian Church located on Oglethorpe Square. Son of the noted Boston reformer, Rev. John Pierpont, he was the brother of Rev. John Pierpont, Jr., minister of this church, and uncle of financier J. Pierpont Morgan. He married Eliza Jane Purse, daughter of Savannah mayor Thomas Purse, and served in a Confederate cavalry regiment. He is buried in Laurel Grove Cemetery, A prolific song- writer, his best known "Jingle Bells" is world famous.

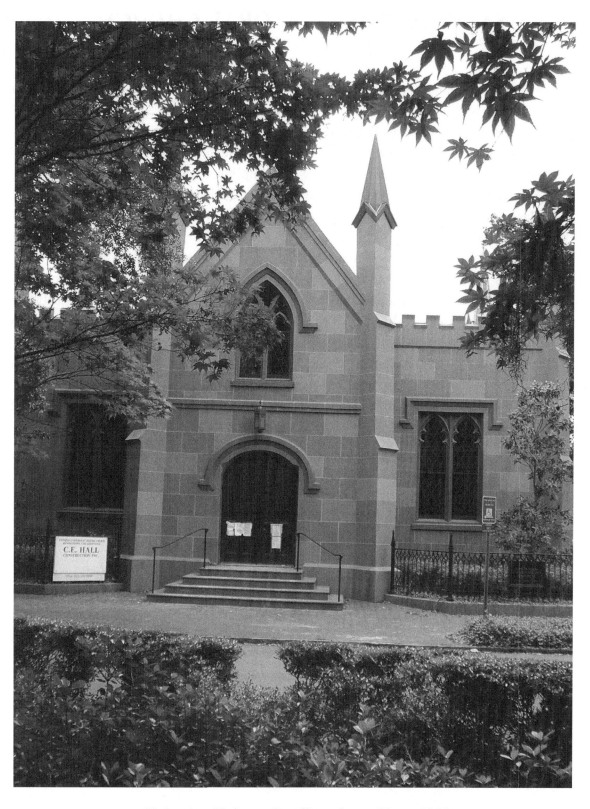

Unitarian Universalist Church   Circa 1851

SAINT JOHN'S EPISCOPAL CHURCH

St. John's Episcopal Church is located at 329 Bull St. in Savannah, GA. in Chatham County. Prominent Buffalo, N.Y. architect Calvin N. Otis designed the church, which was built in 1853 under the supervision of architect Calvin Fay. It was one of the first Gothic Revival churches built in Georgia. The church has pointed arches, buttresses, and great hammerbeam trusses in the interior. A curious part of construction consists of a ship's mast situated in the church's single spire. The church was designed along the lines of a simple English parish house and has a number of stained glass windows depicting various New Testament biblical scenes. The neighborhood has long enjoyed the sound of St. John's bells.

The Green – Meldrim house, which was built for wealthy Savannah cotton merchant Charles Green in 1850 is now the St. John parish house and is separated from the church only by a courtyard. At the time of construction the house was said to have cost $93,000. The building materials including flagstones, laths, planks, etc. were brought to Savannah from England on Mr. Green's ships. The house was designed by the architect John H. Norris of New York. The building was occupied by Union General William Sherman after the capture of Savannah in 1864 at the time he sent his famous telegram to President Lincoln which said, "I beg to present you as a Christmas gift the city of Savannah…" General Sherman's chaplain held Christmas Eve services in the church shortly thereafter.

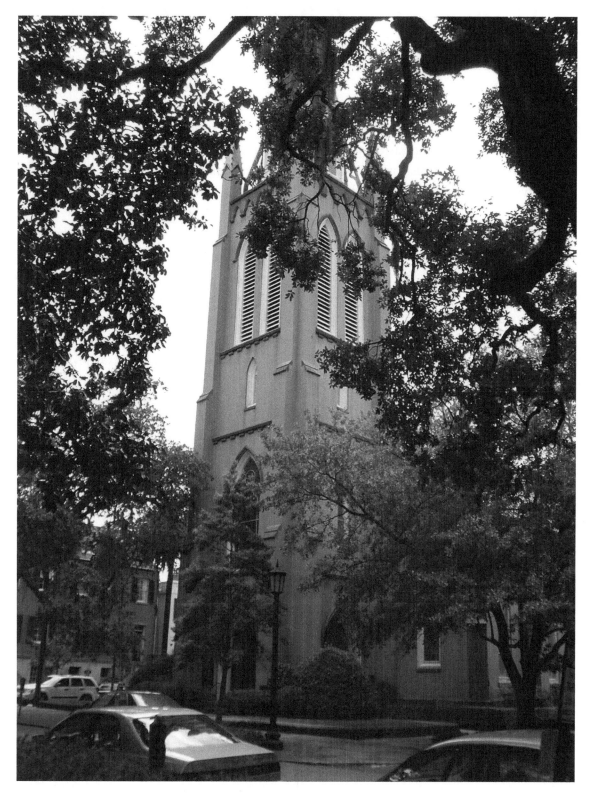

St. John's Episcopal Church   Circa 1853

LUTHERAN CHURCH OF THE ASCENSION

The Evangelical Lutheran Church of the Ascension is located at 120 Bull St. in Savannah, GA. in Chatham County.

The history of this church can be traced back to the beginning of the colony of Georgia. In 1734, a ship brought a group of Austrian Saltzbergers to the new colony. Soon after their arrival, the majority of the Salzbergers, desiring to maintain their own customs and language, petitioned General Oglethorpe for permission to settle west of Savannah in an area they called Ebenezer. Permission was granted and they formed the congregation of New Jerusalem Lutheran Church in Ebenezer.

Those Salzbergers remaining in Savannah formed the congregation of what was to become the Lutheran Church of the Ascension. By 1770 the congregation had grown large enough to seek a more permanent facility and they selected a lot on Wright Square. In 1843 a Greek Revival single-storey building was erected. Thirty-five years later, a second story was added during extensive renovation. As a part of this renovation a huge stained glass window depicting the Ascension was installed and from this time onward, the church has been known as the Lutheran Church of the Ascension. A window on the back wall was installed which portrays Martin Luther before the Diet of Worms.

A GHC marker at the site bears the following inscription:

Lutheran Church of the Ascension
(Founded 1741)

On April 14, 1741, John Martin Bolzius, who as Pastor of the Salzbergers at Ebenezer was in charge of Lutheran work in the colony of Georgia, founded the congregation now known as the Lutheran Church of the Ascension.

In 1756 members of the congregation purchased for one hundred and fifty pounds the lot upon which the present church stands, directly east of this marker. Around 1752 a nearby building which had formerly served as a courthouse was acquired at a cost of seventeen pounds and was moved to this site, becoming the first church building for Lutherans in Savannah.

The present church was erected in 1843. Extensive remodeling was completed in 1879 and at that time it was dedicated as "The Evangelical Lutheran Church of the Ascension." The choice of the name is connected with the beautiful stained glass behind the altar, portraying the Ascension of Christ into heaven.

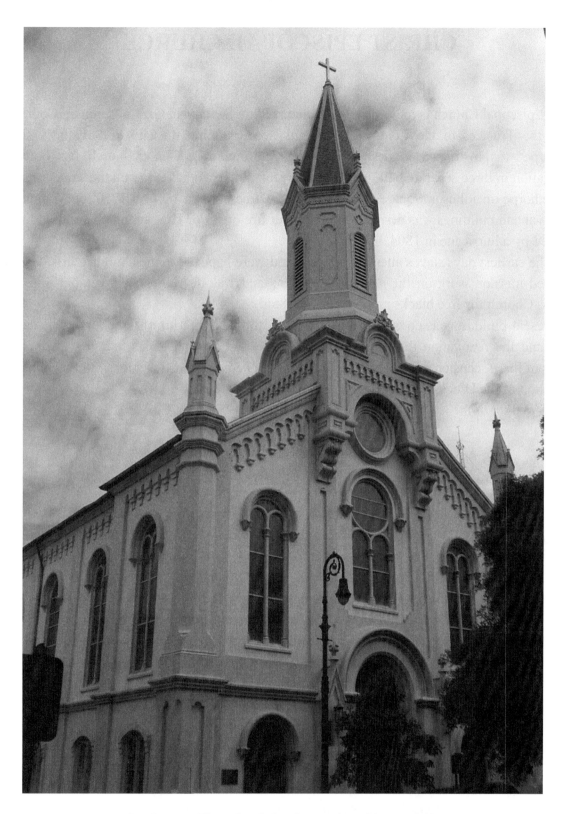

Lutheran Church of the Ascension Circa 1843

CHRIST EPISCOPAL CHURCH

Christ Episcopal Church is located at 18 Abercorn St. in Savannah, GA. in Chatham County.

When the Trustees of the Colony of Georgia were planning the city of Savannah, General Oglethorpe was instructed to designate a site for a church. Christ Church has housed its congregation in three separate buildings over the years, but each has stood on the same lot laid out by Oglethorpe on Johnson Square. The first church structure was built in 1750, but it along with most Savannah buildings was destroyed in the great fire of 1796. The second church building was destroyed by a hurricane in 1804.

From the earliest days slaves attended services and were baptized in the church. Christ Episcopal conducted mission work on the nearby plantations and was instrumental in establishing the St. Stephens Church for free blacks in Savannah in 1856.

The present building was consecrated in 1844. In 1895, the interior of the church was damaged by fire and the renovation that followed created the interior that exists today. A stained glass window of the Ascension installed during that era was dedicated as a memorial to Stephen Elliott, first Bishop of the Diocese of Georgia.

A GHS marker at the site has the following inscription:

Christ Episcopal Church
The Mother Church of Georgia

This Episcopal Church was the first house of worship established with the founding of Georgia in 1733. Early rectors included the Rev. John Wesley (1736-37), who began the earliest form of Sunday school and published the first English Hymnal in the colonies, and the Rev. George Whitefield (1738-40), founder of Bethesda Orphanage. The cornerstone for the first building on this site was laid in 1744. James Hamilton Couper designed the current and third structure in 1838. The 1819 Revere & Son bell continues in use today. One of many prominent members was Juliette Gordon Lowe, founder of the Girl Scouts of America.

A brass marker on the front of the building states: *"The Bell of Christ Church located in the N.E. Tower was built by Paul Revere & Son in 1819 – Weight 1969 lbs."*

An additional brass marker erected on the front of the building states: *"To the Glory of God in loving memory of John Wesley Priest of the Church of England Minister to Savannah 1736-1737 Founder of the Sunday School of this church."*

Christ Episcopal Church   **Circa 1843**

GOSHEN UNITED METHODIST CHURCH

Goshen United Methodist Church is located at 115 Katie Dr. in the city of Rincon, GA. in Effingham County. By all accounts this must be one of the oldest public buildings still standing in Georgia. Tradition states this church was originally located on the banks of the Savannah River between Ebenezer and Savannah. In the 1820's it was sawed in half and moved to its present location.

For more than fifty years this church was pastored by German-speaking Lutheran ministers. It is said that in the 1790's Bishop Asbury was prevailed upon to send Methodist ministers to preach in the church because of this language problem. Within a generation Goshen became a Methodist Church.

A GHC marker at the church site has the following inscription:

Goshen Church

Goshen Church was built about 1751. It was served by the early pastors of the Salzburgers, and later for a short time by the Moravian missionaries. The church remained a part of the Ebenezer Charge until the Revolutionary War.

In 1820 the Methodist Church was organized in Goshen, under the direction of Rev. James O. Andrew, and was allowed to use the Goshen church edifice. The actual deed to the property was transferred to the Methodist Conference several years later. Among the first members of the Goshen Methodist Church were: David Gougle and his daughter; Mrs. Nowlan, wife of Major Nowlan; Major and Mrs. John Charlton.

The Rev. Lewis moved to Goshen about 1823, and served the Methodist Church for many years.

Goshen Methodist Church   Circa 1751

JERUSALEM LUTHERAN CHURCH

Jerusalem Lutheran Church (sometimes referred to as Ebenezer or Old Ebenezer Church) is located at 266 Ebenezer Rd. in Rincon, GA. in Effingham County. The church was first organized in 1733, in Augsburg, Germany by Lutherans who had fled the Saltzburg area of Austria after being expelled on religious grounds by Count Leopold Firmian. Under the leadership of pastors John Boltzius and Israel Gronau, these "Saltzburgers" departed for England where King George II offered them passage to the new colony of Georgia.

General Oglethorpe transported the Saltzburgers to the new colony and settled them in a strategic area using them as a buffer between the Indians and Spanish. This locale proved to be so environmentally hostile that the Salzburgers petitioned Oglethorpe for permission to settle elsewhere. Reluctantly, Oglethorpe granted permission for them to move to an area some twenty miles northwest of Savannah which they called New Ebenezer.

The settlers founded the Jerusalem Evangelical Lutheran Church and the present church building was erected in 1769. The thick sanctuary walls were constructed of brick made from clay dug from the banks of the Savannah River. Descendants of these pioneer settlers still worship in this church making it the oldest continuing congregation in the country. Some of the glass panes in the windows are original.

A wooden marker at the site has the following inscription:

Jerusalem Lutheran Church
Organized in 1734
Built in 1767-69

A GHC marker at the site bears the following inscription:

Jerusalem (Ebenezer) Church

Built in 1767-69 by Lutheran Protestants who came to Georgia in 1734 after being exiled from Catholic Salzburg in Europe, the church is officially named Jerusalem Church. It stands on the site of a wooden building probably erected soon after the congregation moved from Old Ebenezer to New Ebenezer in 1738. During the Revolution the British used the church as a hospital and stable and the metal swan on the belfry still bears a bullet hole. Though the town of Ebenezer no longer exists the church has an active congregation of about 450 members.

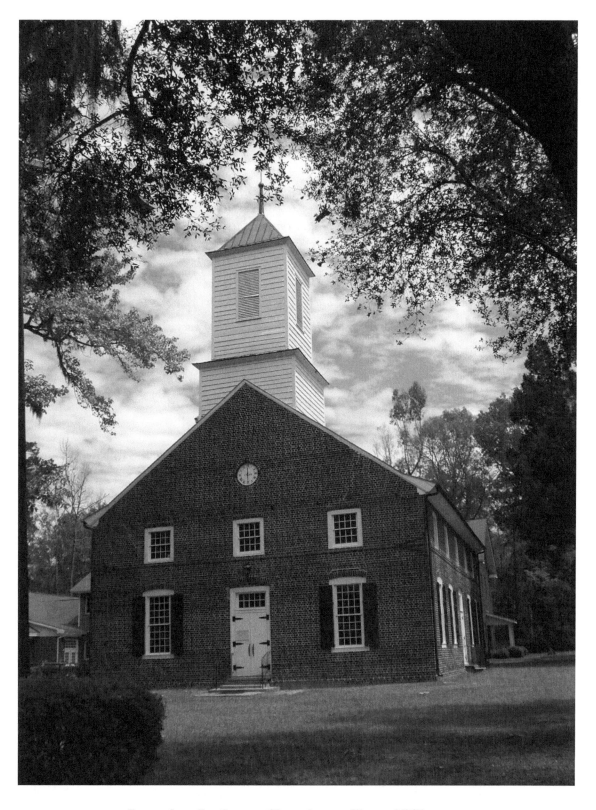

Jerusalem Lutheran Church   Circa 1767

BETHEL METHODIST CHURCH

Bethel (Brick) Church is located two miles northwest of U.S. Highway 301 on Wade Plantation Rd. in Screven County, GA.

A GHC marker at the site has the following inscription:

Brick (Bethel) Church

On Dec. 5, 1827 the Rev. Peyton L. Wade conveyed to John Green, John H. Smith, Robert W. Lovett, Richard Herrington, Sr., Jacob Lewis Elijah Roberts and John H. Nessmith, Trustees, two and three quarter acres of land on which to build a Methodist Episcopal Church to be known as "Brick Church." Construction was started immediately. The building now on site is the original. "Brick Church" was a successor to Lessing's Meeting House, a log building, on nearby Rocky Creek at Scott's Spring.

Rev. John Crawford, who died in 1822, was the founder of Methodism in this community. His widow, Sarah Maner Crawford, married the Rev. Wade in 1823.

A South Georgia Conference (Methodist) marker at the site contains the following inscription:

1827
Bethel United Methodist Church
(Brick Church)

In 1792 Bishop Francis Asbury in his yearly visit to Methodist Societies and Churches in Georgia held services while staying with the Lovetts, owners of Burton Ferry Landing on the Savannah River. In 1811 Bishop Asbury stopped with "David Lovett, Screven Co., preaching on Monday and Wednesday." Robert Watkins Lovett was the first member recorded, 1825. Rev. Payton Wade, a Methodist minister, gave the land and this "brick church" was built in 1827.

"Brick Church" with a parsonage near headed the Bethel Circuit (1858-1897). Since 1897 Bethel has been on the Girard Circuit and is Screven County's oldest continuing Methodist Church.

Bethel (Brick) Methodist Church   Circa 1827

BIG BUCKHEAD BAPTIST CHURCH

Big Buckhead Baptist Church is located in north Jenkins County on Big Buckhead Church Rd. approximately three miles west of Perkins, GA.

This is the third oldest Baptist Church in Georgia having been organized in 1774. The present building is the fourth to occupy the site.

The Georgia Baptist Convention was held here in 1831 and adopted a resolution to establish a classical and theological school known today as Mercer University. Bishop Francis Asbury, first American Bishop of the Methodist Church preached at Buckhead on January 23, 1793.

Tradition claims that the present building was erected and dedicated in 1855 and that pews from the church were used by Confederate cavalry to repair a bridge over Big Buckhead creek that had been partially destroyed by retreating Union forces. After the conflict, the congregation reconstructed the pews and it is said the horses' hoof prints can still be observed in the wood. Big Buckhead Church was the scene of one of the few Confederate victories against Union forces during Gen. Sherman's March through Georgia.

A GHC marker at the site has the following inscription:

Big Buckhead Church

This church, near Buckhead Creek, from which it derives its name, was probably organized before the Revolution by Matthew Moore, Baptist minister, whose loyalist sympathies led him to leave with the British. Buckhead Church was reconstituted Sept. 11, 1787 with James Matthews, pastor, and Sanders Walker and Josiah Taylor acting with him as presbytery. Four church buildings have stood on or near this site. The first was log, followed in 1807 by a white frame one. A brick church was built in 1830. It was condemned and the present one was erected. Here the Hephzibah Assn was organized and plans to create Mercer Univ. proposed.

Big Buckhead Baptist Church   Circa 1855

FIRST PRESBYTERIAN CHURCH OF AUGUSTA

The First Presbyterian Church of Augusta is located on Telfair St. in the city of Augusta, GA., in Richmond County. Around 1796 a one acre lot was given to the Presbyterians on which to build a church. As originally incorporated, the new building was called Christ Church, but by legislative act in 1836, this name was changed to First Presbyterian Church.

During the Civil War, the First Presbyterian Church, by virtue of its closeness to the railroad, was utilized as a Confederate hospital. It was from this church that the funeral for famed Confederate General W.H.T. Walker, killed during the Battle of Atlanta, was held. He is buried in Augusta. Reportedly, young Woodrow Wilson was a witness to Union soldiers escorting captured Confederate President Jefferson Davis through Augusta from his vantage point across the street from the church.

In the War Between the States the church and grounds were used as part of a military hospital and a temporary detention center for prisoners of war.

The building was renovated in 1896. The Telfair Building was added in 1881 for Sunday school classes. New Sunday school addition was made in the1950s.

A GHC marker at the site bears the following inscription:

The First Presbyterian Church

Organized by the Rev. Washington McKnight, rector of Richmond Academy, in 1804. Met at first at the site of St. Paul's Church. Incorporated by the Georgia General Assembly and given a lot on the common by Richmond Academy Trustees. Cornerstone of the present church laid July 4, 1809. Building dedicated May 17, 1812. Spire added in 1818. An outstanding pastor was the Rev. Joseph R. Wilson, 1850-1870, father of Woodrow Wilson. December 4, 1861, the General Assembly of the Presbyterian Church was organized here.

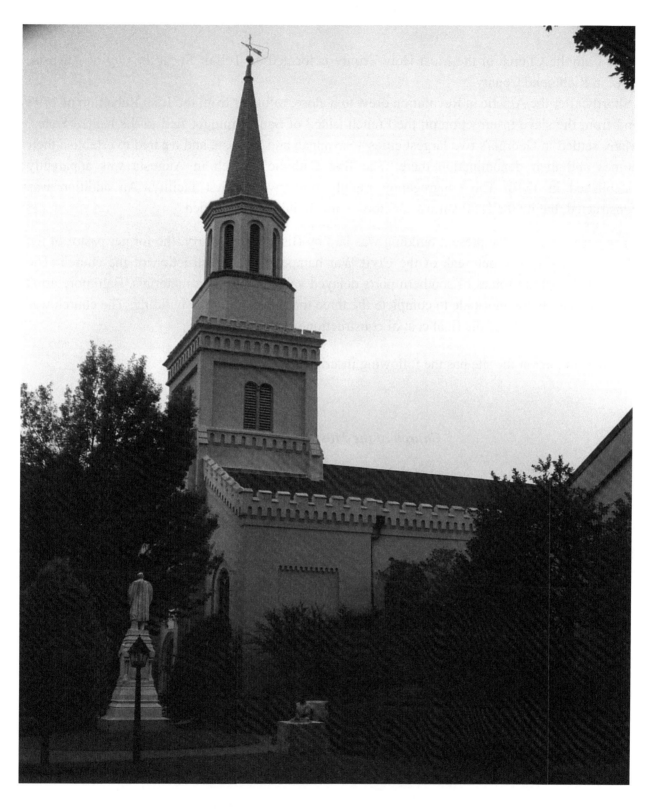

First Presbyterian Church of Augusta   Circa 1809

61

CHURCH OF THE MOST HOLY TRINITY

The Catholic Church of the Most Holy Trinity is located on Telfair St. in the city of Augusta, GA., in Richmond County.

Shortly after the American Revolution drew to a close, refugees from the Irish Rebellion of 1798 and from the slave insurrection on the French island of San Domingo, fled to the United States. Many settled in Georgia's two largest cities - Savannah and Augusta and desired to establish their homes and their denomination there. The first Catholic Church in Augusta was apparently established in 1810. The congregation rapidly outgrew the first facility. An addition was constructed, but by the 1850's it was obvious a new building was needed.

The cornerstone of the present building was laid by Bishop John Barry, the former pastor of the church, in 1857. The outbreak of the Civil War hampered the construction of the church. The blockade by Union forces of southern ports delayed valuable building materials. Baltimore artist John Mullen ran the blockade to complete the three marble altars in the building. The church was consecrated in 1863 and the final cost of construction was $42,833.32.

A GHC marker at the site has the following inscription:

Church of the Most Holy Trinity

The current sanctuary was constructed from 1857-63 and is one of the oldest Catholic Church buildings in Georgia. It was designed by J.R. Niernsee, architect of the State House in Columbia, South Carolina. The original 1814 structure served as the Sisters of Mercy hospital and orphanage during the yellow fever epidemic of 1839 and 1854. It was again used as their hospital during the Civil War. Father Abram Ryan (1838-1886), "poet-priest of the Confederacy," edited the Banner of the South, a Catholic weekly, while serving as pastor of the church during the Civil War.

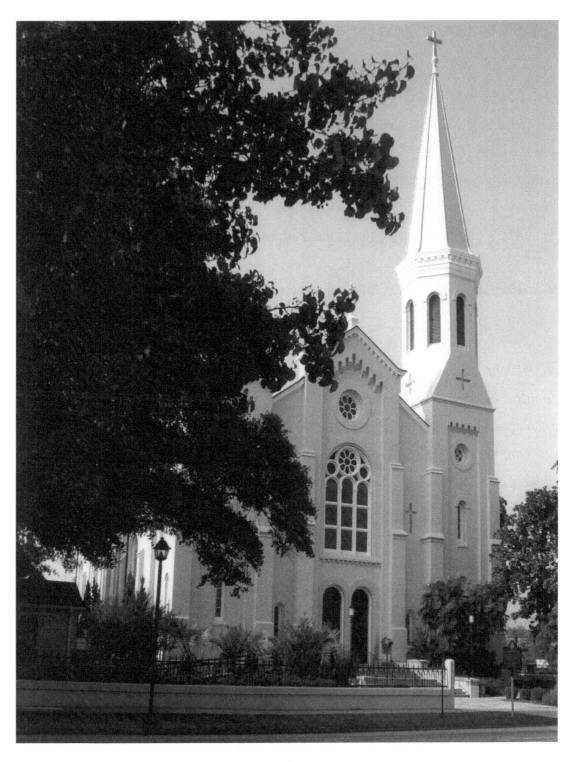

Church of the Most Holy Trinity   **Circa 1857**

SAINT JOHN METHODIST CHURCH

Saint John Methodist Church is located on Greene St. in the city of Augusta in Richmond County. The original Methodist church was built on 'Stith Mead's' lot on Greene St. in 1801 and was called Asbury Chapel. The pastor at this time was the Rev. John Garvis. When the congregation outgrew this building, a new, large brick church was erected in 1844 and was named Saint John Methodist. From St. John's so many new Methodist congregations were established that the church is known with affection as the `Mother of Churches.'

A GHC marker at the site has the following inscription:

Two Early Augusta Churches

St. John Methodist Church was founded in 1798 by Stith Mead, a young Virginia minister who denounced the worldliness of fun-loving Augusta. Bishop Francis Asbury visited the church and watched its growth with particular interest. Augustus B. Longstreet and five Methodist Bishops, including James O. Andrew, George F. Pierce and Warren A. Candler, were pastors of St. John. Lorenzo Dow, the colorful and eccentric evangelist, also figured in the early history of the church. In 1844, the original church building, constructed in 1801, began a new phase of its ecclesiastical history when it was sold to another early congregation, the Springfield Baptist Church. The structure was moved to the S.E. corner of Reynolds and Marbury- where for approximately 50 years before, members of what is usually considered the first Negro Baptist Church in America at Silver Bluff, South Carolina had worshipped after they fled with their masters to Augusta when the British occupied Silver Bluff in 1778. These Silver Bluff – refugee- charter members of the circa 1790 Springfield Baptist congregation, account for its claim that it is one of the oldest, if not the oldest active Negro Baptist congregation in the United States.

St. John Methodist Church   Circa 1844

SPRINGFIELD BAPTIST CHURCH

Springfield Baptist Church is located at the corner of 12th St. and Reynolds St. in the city of Augusta, GA., in Richmond County. The white frame building is one of the oldest church facilities in the state.

Springfield traces its roots to the year 1773 and claims to be the oldest African American congregation in the United States. It was served by African American pastors during the antebellum period. Some of its members immigrated to Liberia and Springfield maintained a missionary connection with that country for many years.

A GHC marker at the site contains the following inscription:

Springfield Baptist Church
Birthplace of Morehouse College

This building, which was erected in 1801 by Augusta's first Methodist Society, was moved to this location in 1844 to become the home of Springfield Baptist Church. Organized in 1787 by Jessie Peters, the Springfield Baptist Church is the oldest independent African-American Church in the nation. This church helped bridge the transition between slavery and free citizenship and has stood as a focus for black community life.

This church building is the major landmark remaining from the free-black community of Springfield. The original structure was moved to the rear of the lot when the new brick building was built in 1897. Springfield Church helped establish many black institutions.

In 1867, Morehouse College, the nation's only all-male, historically black undergraduate institution, was founded in the basement of Springfield Baptist Church by Richard Cooper and Edmund Tumey, while Henry Watts was serving as pastor. The school moved to Atlanta in 1879 and was renamed Morehouse College in 1913. This marker unveiled February 16, 1992, commemorates the 125th anniversary of Morehouse College's founding.

Springfield Baptist Church   Circa 1801

HEPHZIBAH METHODIST CHURCH

Hephzibah Methodist Church is located at the corner of Church St. and Brothersville Rd. in Hephzibah, GA., in Richmond County.

A GHC marker at the site has the following inscription:

Hephzibah Methodist Church

The Brothersville Methodist Church was organized in March 1852 in the community of Brothersville to serve the fifteen families living there. The building, completed in 1853, was dedicated in 1854 By Bishop George Pierce. In 1890 the church was moved a short distance to the village of Hephzibah and later the name was changed to Hephzibah Methodist Church. Many outstanding citizens have gone from its ranks to other communities. Among them are Rev. Milton Anthony Clark, for thirty years a missionary to the Indians in Oklahoma, and Rev. W.H. Clark.

Hephzibah Methodist Church   Circa 1853

KIOKEE BAPTIST CHURCH

The `Old Kiokee' Baptist Church is located at 6145 Tubman Rd., north of Georgia Highway 104 in Columbia County, GA., near the Kiokee Creek. The church is active today in a different facility called `New Kiokee' Baptist Church located about three miles from the old brick building. The congregation joined the first association of Georgia Baptists and the church was active in missionary work in the Augusta area. The first pastor, Daniel Marshall, was succeeded by his son, Abraham in 1784 and was upon his death succeeded by his son, Jabez in 1819. Father, son and grandfather, the Marshalls had provided pastoral care for the Kiokee congregation for some sixty years.

A marker erected by the Georgia Baptist Convention has the following inscription:

Kiokee Baptist Church

The oldest Baptist church in Georgia, constituted in the spring of 1772 by Daniel Marshall and served by him as pastor until his death in 1784, was originally located a few yards southwest from this marker as described in courthouse records of Columbia County. Church was removed in 1808 to brick building three miles away which still stands. Present church is located in Appling.

A GHC marker which stands before the Columbia County Courthouse in Appling, GA. reads in part as follows:

Columbia County

Columbia County, named for Christopher Columbus, was created by Act of Dec. 10, 1790 from Richmond County. Originally, it contained parts of McDuffie and Warren Counties. Settled by Quakers before the Revolution, it has been the home of many prominent Georgians. Here were Carmel Academy and Kiokee Baptist Church, "Mother Church" of Baptists in Georgia...

Kiokee Baptist Church   Circa 1808

SHILOH METHODIST CHURCH

Shiloh Methodist Church is situated on Georgia Highway 150 approximately 12 miles from the city of Thomson in Columbia County, GA. It began like so many early Georgia churches did with a congregation gathering by a spring in a brush arbor to hold worship services. Soon there was an expressed desire to build a more permanent facility. In 1858 the church trustees paid $380.96 for materials to construct the present building. One third of the new building was set apart for slaves.

A GHC marker at the site contains the following inscription:

Shiloh Methodist Church

Shiloh Methodist Church, the outgrowth of the earliest known Methodist place of worship in this community, has had a church building on this site for over 125 years. Originally, services started by a local hermit "who lived by a spring," were held in a "brush arbor" about a mile west of here. A short time later a church was built on this site. In Sept. 1825, after the church was completed, two plots of land were deeded to the four commissioners of the Methodist meeting house, One, including the hermit's spring, was from Waters Briscoe, the other, including the site of Shiloh Church, was from Green Dozier. The present church building was erected in 1859 .

Shiloh Methodist Church   **Circa 1858**

WRIGHTSBORO METHODIST CHURCH

The Wrightsboro Methodist Church is located on Wrightsboro Rd. some nine miles north of the City of Thomson, GA. in McDuffie County.

The town of Wrightsboro was founded by Quakers in 1769. It has been called the oldest, continually occupied community in the interior of Georgia although the town itself no longer exists.

The first Quaker Meeting House was built in 1773. In 1799 two lots were set aside for a church cemetery where the present building is now located. Early records indicate the present building was erected between 1810 and 1812 by public subscription. In 1877 the Methodists successfully petitioned the town for the deed to the church since they had exclusively maintained and operated the building since the 1830's. The Methodists maintained possession until the congregation was disbanded in 1964 and the property was conveyed to McDuffie County.

A GHC marker at the site has the following inscription:

Wrightsboro Methodist Church

The Wrightsboro Methodist Church of the Thomson Circuit, on the site of the dead town of Wrightsboro, has been an active organization for over 125 years. In its historic churchyard are buried several veterans of the Revolutionary War and some who died at Gettysburg, Shiloh and Fredericksburg in the War Between the States. The founders of some of the most prominent Georgia families are buried here. Among them are Theodosius Erwin Massengale, grandfather of St. Elmo Massengale, and the ancestors of Bishop Warren A. Candler, Judge John S. Candler and Asa G. Candler.

Wrightsboro Methodist Church   **Circa 1810**

LINCOLNTON PRESBYTERIAN CHURCH

The Lincolnton Presbyterian Church is located on N. Washington St. in the town of Lincolnton, GA. in Lincoln County. Originally called the Old Union Church, it was built shortly after the land was obtained from Peter Lamar in 1823. This building was the first and only church in Lincolnton until after 1870. It is said that Methodists, Baptists and Presbyterians originally used the church on alternate weeks.

Lincolnton Presbyterian Church   Circa 1825

GOSHEN BAPTIST CHURCH

Goshen Baptist Church is located on Goshen Church Rd. in Lincoln County, GA.

The pioneer families of sparsely settled Lincoln County, lacking the financial resources to build separate churches for the Methodists, Baptists and Presbyterians, elected to band together to build a common house of worship to serve their community. In 1797 Goshen Church was constituted. As the community grew, so did each of these congregations and by 1835, the Baptists decided to build their own church and this building is today the sanctuary for Goshen Baptist Church.

The church was constructed using native pine for the most part and the sixty foot sleepers and sills were hand hewn and the axe prints of the builders are still visible today. The original rafters were thirty seven feet long.

Like most southern churches of the antebellum period, the Goshen Baptist Church congregation included both black and white members. In 1863 the membership consisted of twenty four whites and one hundred seventeen blacks.

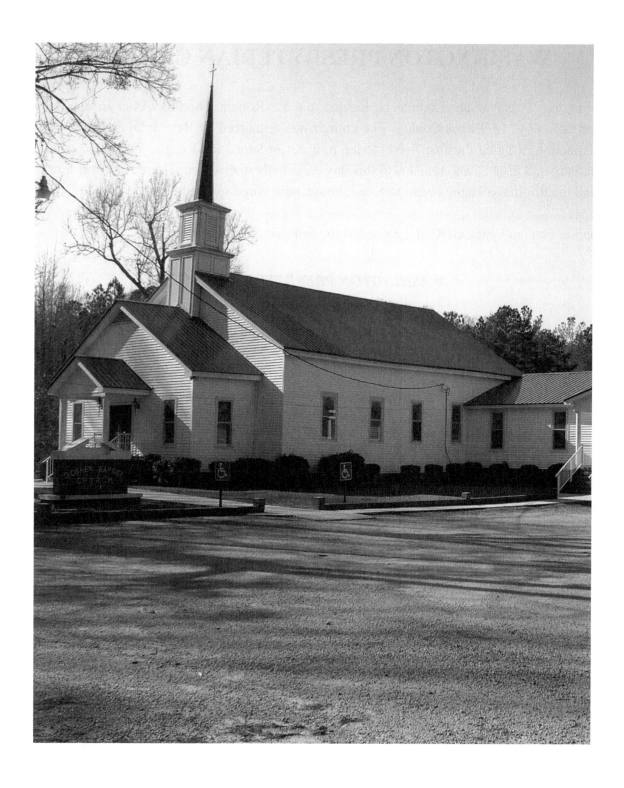

Goshen Baptist Church   **Circa 1835**

WASHINGTON PRESBYTERIAN CHURCH

Washington Presbyterian Church is located on E. Robert Toombs Ave. in the city of Washington, GA., in Wilkes County. The church was organized by Rev. John Springer who has the distinction of being the first Presbyterian minister ordained in Georgia. The present building was constructed in 1825 and remains to this day essentially unchanged. There is a choir loft in the rear and the original oil lamps were retained though now wired for electricity.

A marker erected by the GHC at the site has the following inscription:

WASHINGTON PRESBYTERIAN CHURCH

The Presbyterian Church at Washington was organized in 1790, under the Presbytery of South Carolina, with the Rev. John Springer as first pastor. Services were held in private homes, in the Court House, the Academy and in the Methodist Church, until 1825, when the first church edifice was erected. On July 29, of that year, the lot upon which the present church building stands was conveyed by Dr. Joel Abbott to Thomas Terrell, Samuel Barnett, Andrew G. Semmes, Constantine Church and James Wingfield, Trustees of Washington Presbyterian Church.

The Georgia Presbytery was organized at a meeting of the South Carolina and Georgia Synod in Washington in 1821, and in 1826 the Synod met in the new church building. Many famous ministers have been pastors of the Washington Presbyterian Church, among them: the Rev. Alexander H. Webster, the Rev. S.J. Cassells, the Rev. Francis R. Goulding, the Rev. John Brown, the Rev. H.W. Petrie, the Rev. Nathan Hoyt, the Rev. J.K.S. Axson and the Rev. Thomas Dunwoody. Alexander H. Stephens and Duncan G. Campbell were lifelong members of this church as were also many other distinguished men and women.

Washington Presbyterian Church Circa 1825

SOUTH LIBERTY PRESBYTERIAN CHURCH

South Liberty Presbyterian Church is located on Georgia Highway 269 in the town of Sharon, GA., in Taliferro County. It is believed the present structure is the original 1855 building.

A GHC marker at the site contains the following inscription:

South Liberty Presbyterian Church

In 1820, several members of Liberty Church, Wilkes County, petitioned to form a new church, South Liberty, because of "distance, bad roads, and high water in winter." A log church was built in 1828 about 4 miles east of Sharon on land given by Joshua Morgan. Services began in May 1828 and were held continually except during the War Between the States when the minister and members were on military duty. In 1855 the log church was replaced by a frame building and, in 1877 that was moved to the present location in Sharon. First elders were Moses Alexander, C.C. Mills, and Joshua Morgan. Dr. Carlyle P. Bemon was the first minister.

South Liberty Presbyterian Church

South Liberty Presbyterian Church   **Circa 1855**

POWELTON BAPTIST CHURCH

Powelton Baptist Church is located on Ga. Highway 22 in the Powelton Community in Hancock County. The second pastor, Rev. Jesse Mercer, founded Penfield Institute, which later became Mercer University in Macon, GA. The church is currently being renovated.

A marker erected in 1950 by the Georgia Baptist Convention contains the following inscription:

Powelton Baptist Church

In this church on this site the General Baptist Association of Georgia was organized June 27, 1822, by messengers from the Georgia and Ocmulgee Associations and certain other Baptists, including Adiel Sherwood, whose motion in the Sarepta Association called for organization of the General Association. Jessie Mercer was elected president and Jabez P. Marshall was elected secretary. Adiel Sherwood preached the sermon, Luke 3:4. Name changed to The Baptist Convention of the State of Georgia in 1827.

A GHC marker at the site has the following inscription:

Powelton Baptist Church

The Powelton Baptist Church, first known as Powell's Creek Church, was constituted July 1st, 1786, with 26 members, by the Rev. John Harvey and the Rev. John Thomas. The Rev. Jesse Mercer became pastor of this church on February 4, 1797, and served in that capacity until late in 1825. During his ministry, 200 members were baptized into the church.

The General Committee of the Georgia Baptists was organized here in 1803; the Baptist State Convention was formed in this church in 1822, and its sessions were held here in 1823 and 1832.

Governor William Rabun was a distinguished member of Powelton Baptist Church and served it as Clerk and Chorister.

Powelton Baptist Church   **Circa 1820**

BETHESDA BAPTIST CHURCH

This church is located about five miles northeast of Union Point in Greene County, GA., on Bethesda Church Rd. It is one of the oldest brick church buildings in Georgia.

Jessie Mercer, one of Georgia's most prominent ministers of the early 19th century, was born in North Carolina in 1769. He was the son of Rev. Silas Mercer who moved to Wilkes County in the early 1770's and founded several pioneer Baptist churches. He baptized his son, Jessie, at the age of eighteen and the youth was ordained a minister at the age of nineteen. Jessie succeeded his father as pastor of Phillip's Mill in 1796. He also served as pastor of Bethesda (1797-1827), Powell's Creek (1797-1825), the Baptist Church in Edenton (1820-1826), and Washington Baptist Church 1828-1841). He was the founder of Mercer Institute at Penfield which later was moved to Macon, GA., and became Mercer University

A GHC marker at the site contains the following inscription:

Bethesda Baptist Church

When Bethesda Baptist Church was organized in 1785, it was known as Whatley's Mill Church, and was in Wilkes County before it was added to Greene in 1802. When the present building was erected in 1818, the name was changed to Bethesda. Jessie Mercer was pastor for a number of years and here he ordained Adiel Sherwood as minister of the Gospel. This splendid brick structure indicates that this section was populous and wealthy. In the early days of the church, worshipers, fearful of attack by the Indians, carried their guns to services.

A marble marker placed in front of the church bears the following inscription:

Bethesda Baptist Church

Est. 1785

Building Erected 1818

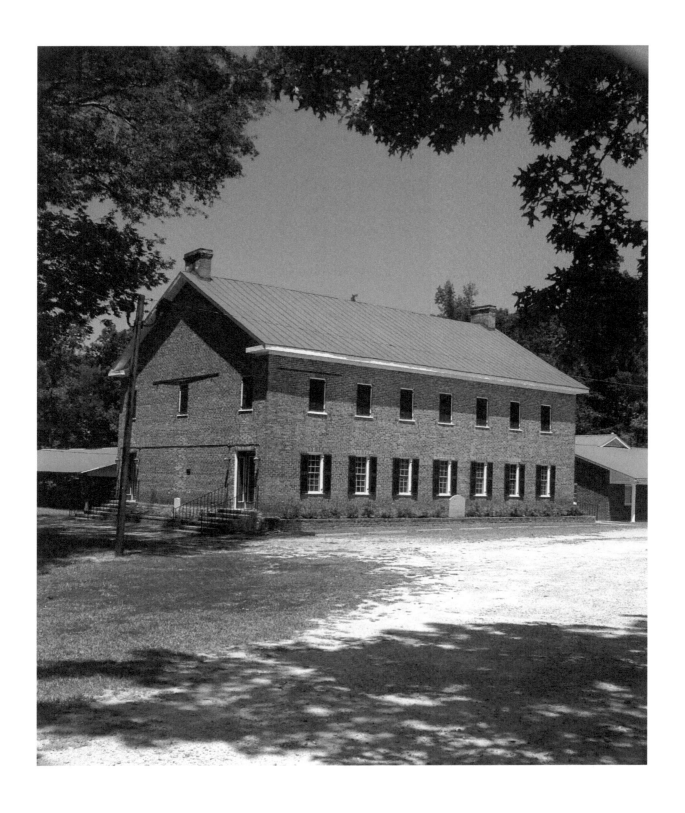

Bethesda Baptist Church   **Circa 1818**

PENFIELD BAPTIST CHURCH

Penfield Baptist Church, formerly known as Penfield Chapel, is located on Penfield Rd. in the community of Penfield, GA. in Greene County.

A GHC marker at the site bears the following inscription:

"Old Mercer"

Actuated by a legacy from Josiah Penfield, Mercer University was founded here in 1833 as Mercer Institute. After considering several locations, the Trustees moved the institution to Macon in 1871 and, in 1880, transferred all holdings in Penfield to the Georgia Baptist Association, except the venerable Penfield Cemetery where Jessie Mercer, Billington M. Sanders, Mrs. Sanders, and other notable Mercerians are buried. The chapel was given to the Penfield Baptist Church, founded in 1839 with Rev. Adiel Sherwood as pastor. The academy building became the Penfield public school building.

A bronze plaque attached to the church has the following inscription:

The Penfield Chapel
Mercer University
Erected 1846
Restored 1949

This historic building – one of the finest patterns of classic Revival architecture in the South – cherished by Georgia Baptists as a symbol of the faith and vision of the Founding Fathers – was restored and rededicated by the Georgia Baptist Convention and the Penfield Baptist Church on November 17, 1949 on which occasion the closing period of the 128th Annual Session of the Convention was held in this building.

This plaque presented by the Druid Hills Baptist Church.

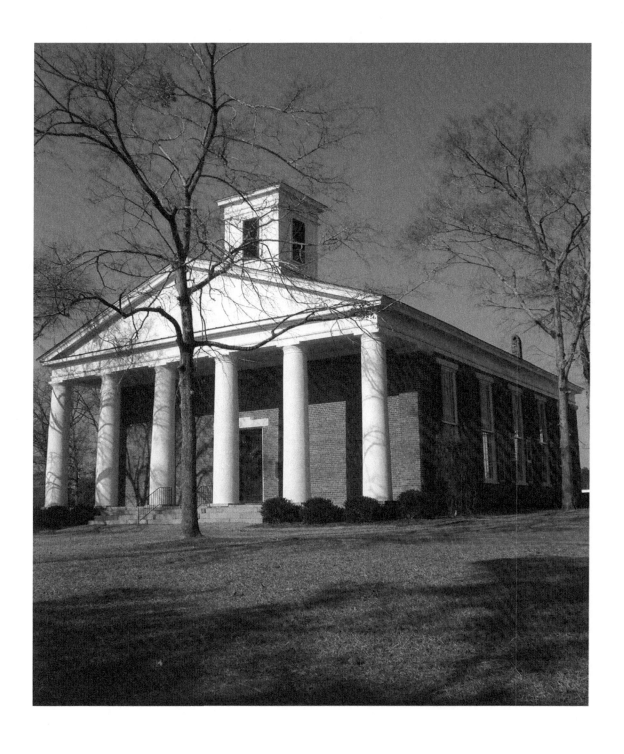

Penfield Baptist Church   **Circa 1846**

MADISON PRESBYTERIAN CHURCH

Madison Presbyterian Church is located on South Main St. in the city of Madison in Morgan County, GA.

In the first decades of the eighteenth century, Presbyterians in Madison attended worship services in the county courthouse. The Madison Presbyterian Church was organized in 1821. The Elders of the church purchased the present site for the church from Jacob Rule who had used the property for his residence, a carriage house and a blacksmith shop. A stipulation in the church charter states that no part of the property can be used as a cemetery.

The present building was erected in 1842 under the supervision of Daniel Killian, a master mason. The church is Greek Revival in style with a square belfry. It has three entrance doors. A gallery was built for slaves who entered from the outside.

Alexander H. Stephens, Vice President of the Confederacy and Governor of Georgia once worshipped here. President Woodrow Wilson's first wife, Ellen Axson, was the daughter of Rev. Samuel Axson who was minister of this church in 1866 and 1867.

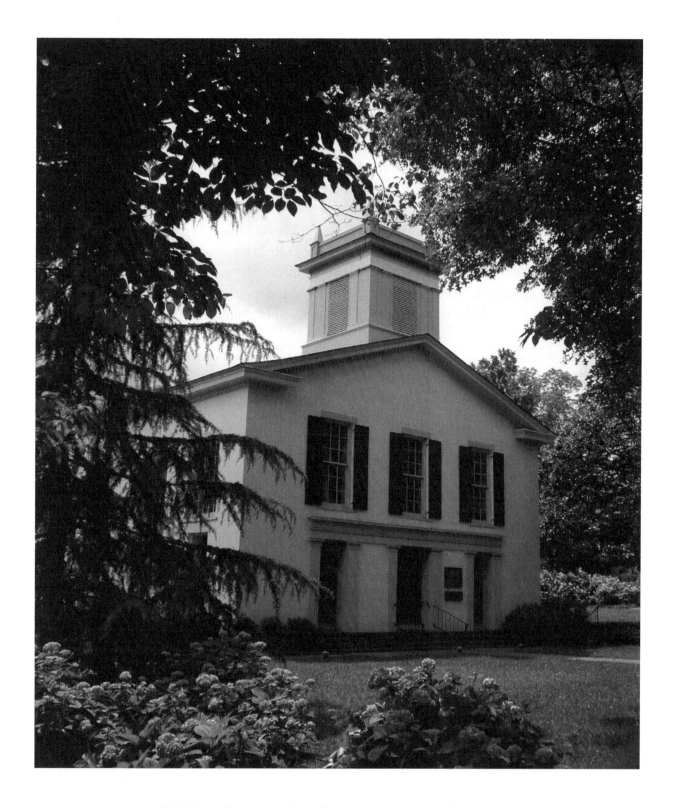

Madison Presbyterian Church   **Circa 1842**

THE CHURCH OF THE ADVENT

The Episcopal Church of the Advent is located on Academy St. in the city of Madison in Morgan County, GA. This building is one of Madison's earliest church structures and was erected in 1840. For many years this brick building served as Madison's Methodist Church before their new building was erected in 1914. The Christian Scientists bought the building and used it as their place of worship for several decades. Later the Episcopalians purchased and renovated the historic building modeling the interior after the style of the old Episcopal Church in Williamsburg, VA. The present choir loft was originally used as a slave gallery.

It is believed that Episcopalians held worship services in the Morgan County Courthouse and in various members' homes as early as 1848. In 1851 a group of Episcopalians petitioned the Superior Court for the purpose of establishing a church to be known as the Advent Church of Madison.

In 1843 a small, Greek Revival building that could seat forty people was consecrated by Bishop Stephen Elliott, Jr., the first Episcopal Bishop of Georgia. Declining membership contributed to the neglect of the building until by the 1930's vagrants had rendered the church unfit for use. In 1937 it was sold to the City of Madison for $250 and was torn down.

Episcopalians purchased the old Methodist building in 1961 and Episcopalian Bishop Randolph Claiborne consecrated it as the Church of the Advent in 1963.

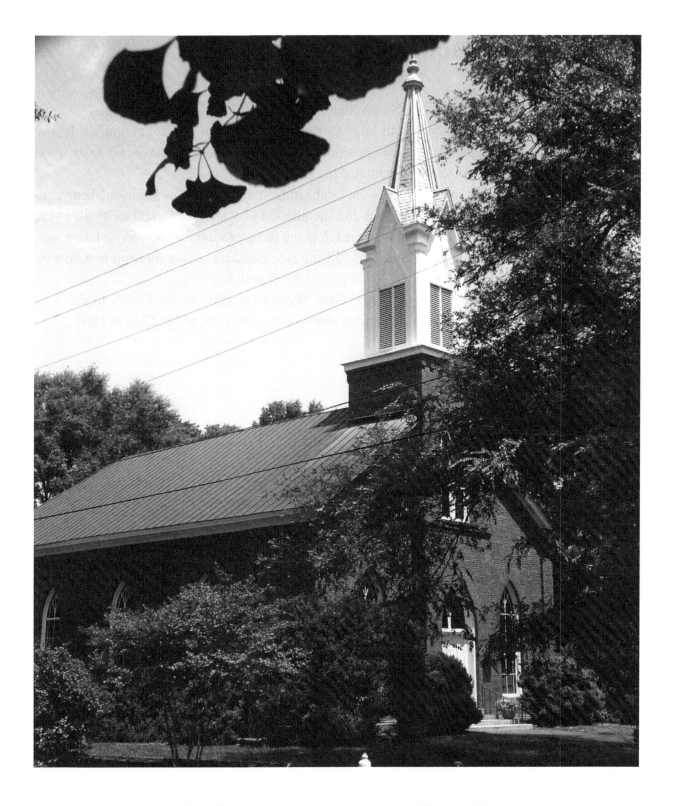

The Church of the Advent   Circa 1840

MADISON BAPTIST CHURCH

Madison Baptist Church is located on South Main St. in the city of Madison in Morgan County, GA. It is an imposing brick structure with large Corinthian columns at the front entrance. It was built in 1858 and the bricks used in its construction were manufactured by slaves on John Byne Walker's plantation. It is said each brick contains his initials, J.B.W.

In 1834 a group of Baptists met to discuss the establishment of a church in Madison. Ten years later, it was reported that the church claimed 237 members, 147 whites and 120 blacks. In 1849, H.G. Foster was the first ordained minister to preach to the congregation. In 1854 a resolution was passed to build a new church facility and by 1858 the new building was completed at a cost of $11,536.89. The gallery built for slaves is still a part of the church building.

Tradition relates that Union Calvary, part of Gen. Sherman's army on his March to the Sea, stabled their horses in the basement of the church during the occupation of Madison in 1864.

Madison Baptist Church   **Circa 1858**

FIRST PRESBYTERIAN CHURCH OF ATHENS

The First Presbyterian Church is located on Hancock St. in the city of Athens, GA. in Clarke County. The first church building was erected in 1828 and served the congregation until the present building was constructed in 1855-56 at a cost of $10,000.

A GHC marker at the site contains the following inscription:

Dr. Moses Waddell
Noted Educator and
Presbyterian Minister

Dr. Moses Waddell, educator and minister, was born in 1770 in N.C. At fourteen he began teaching pupils near his home. Moving to Georgia in 1786, he taught in the Greensboro area until 1787, opening another school at Bethany, Greene County, in 1788. While at Bethany Waddell decided to enter the ministry. He studied at Hampton-Sydney College and graduated in less than nine months in 1791, thereafter combining the careers of teacher and minister.

Establishing his most famous academy at Willington, S.C., in 1804, Waddell continued his work there until 1819 when he became president of Franklin College, now the University of Georgia. One of the most prominent ante-bellum leaders of that institution, he served until 1829. Unwilling to divorce education from religion, Waddell stimulated the religious life of the campus. In 1820 he organized and was pastor of the First Presbyterian Church. The present church building was erected in 1855.

Waddell died in 1840 at his son's home in Athens. His pupils during a lifetime of teaching included John. C. Calhoun, William H. Crawford, George R. Gilmer, Augustus B. Longstreet and George McDuffie.

First Presbyterian Church of Athens   Circa 1855

UNIVERSITY CHAPEL

The University Chapel is located on the "old" campus of the University Of Georgia in the city of Athens, GA. in Clarke County.

In 1830 a terrible fire destroyed one of the only two large buildings located on the University of Georgia campus. Lost were all scientific equipment and the college library that had been so carefully assembled during the first thirty years of the university's existence.

Trustees of the university, having no money to rebuild, appealed to the Georgia Legislature and were granted an immediate loan of $10,000. In addition, they were assured of an annual appropriation of $6,000 which continued for eleven years.

In August 1831, the Trustees approved the construction of a new chapel for the college with the contract being awarded to James R. Carlton and Benjamin Towns. One year later, the Trustees are recorded as proclaiming, "The new chapel which is nearly complete is a tasteful and handsome building. It is apparently correct in its proportions; it is certainly elegant in its exterior appearance and convenient in its interior."

When it was finished, this classical building was one of the finest structures not only in the state, but also in the entire South. In the early days of our country, the Protestant faith was predominant in colleges and universities throughout the nation including the University of Georgia. As in so many other state colleges, the Chapel became a center for student activities. Students were required to attend religious services in the Chapel and assemblies and commencement activities were held in the building for many years.

University Chapel   Circa 1832

COVINGTON FIRST UNITED METHODIST CHURCH

Covington First United Methodist Church is located on Conyers St. in the city of Covington, GA. in Newton County. This is the third structure built by the First Methodist Church in Covington. The second structure, built in 1830, still exists and was moved to a site on Usher St. and is now known as Bethlehem Baptist Church.

In 1860, this site was purchased and the present building was designed and built in the French Renaissance style. Shortly after its completion and dedication, a renowned evangelist, Habersham Evans, led a revival and many new members were reported to have been added to the church roll.

During the Civil War and, more particularly, during the Battle of Atlanta, this building was used as a hospital for wounded Confederate soldiers. Church records indicate that Pressley Jones, a member of the congregation, was killed by Union raiders on July 22, 1864.

The building was extensively renovated in 1897 and the large Sunday school building was erected in 1911.

The imposing front entrance with its huge columns impressed Hollywood when the movie 'A Man Called Peter' was in the planning stage. The church was selected to represent Peter Marshall's Atlanta church when filming began.

Distinguished Methodist Bishops who preached from the pulpit of this church include Atticus Hagood and Warren Candler.

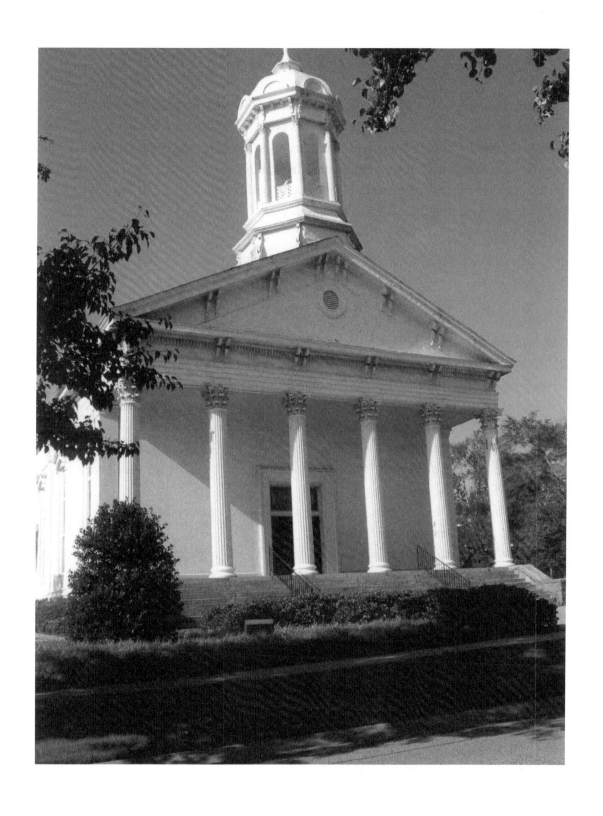

Covington Methodist Church   Circa 1860

OLD OXFORD METHODIST CHURCH

What is now affectionately called Old Church is located on Wesley Street in the City of Oxford, Ga. in Newton County. Matthew Raiford was pastor when the present church was erected in 1841. Bishop William Capers who preached the first commencement sermon of the college in the new church that same year dedicated the building on June 23, 1841. The building was used as the community church as well as for special college activities. During the Civil War the building was used as a Confederate Hospital.

A Newton County Historical Society marker at the site contains the following inscription:

Old Church

Old Church was the first Chapel of Emory College, and the Church for Methodists in Oxford, a pulpit for scholar preachers. It was the center for Methodism in the South when the issue of slavery split the Church in 1844, contributing to the secession of Southern states. It was used as an infirmary during the Civil War. The Church remained a regular place of worship until 1910. 1932-1936 --- Recognized as a historic landmark by DAR 1949 - Final session of Annual Conference held in Old Church 1972 - Oxford designated a Heritage Landmark by the United Methodist Church
1974 - Oxford Historical Shrine Society, Inc. assumed responsibility
for property located on City land.
1975 - Oxford Historic District listed on National Register of Historic Places.

The inscription below is taken from a stone marker on the church grounds.

The Old Oxford Church erected 1841

Restored in 1949 under the direction of Bishop Arthur J. Moore

A symbol of our Father's face, scene of many historic occasions,

Loved by many generations of Emory students

It was for many, another Bethel, the house of God, the Gate of Heaven.

"Move not the ancient landmark." Proverbs 22:28

Old Oxford Methodist Church   Circa 1841

BETHLEHEM BAPTIST CHURCH

Bethlehem Baptist Church is located at 2177 Usher St. in the city of Covington, GA. in Newton County. This building is one of the oldest churches still standing in the state. It was built in 1830 and was originally located at Washington St. and Lee St. where it housed the First Methodist congregation. When the Methodists built a new church in 1860, this building was moved to Usher St. and became the Bethlehem Baptist Church. Originally a frame structure, the building now has a brick façade. One of the prominent ministers of this church was the Rev. A.V. Williams, the grandfather of Dr. Martin Luther King Jr.

Bethlehem Baptist Church   **Circa 1830**

HOPEWELL ASSOCIATE REFORMED PRESBYTERIAN CHURCH

Hopewell Associate Reformed Presbyterian Church is located on Hopewell Church Rd. in Newton County, GA. Pioneer families from South Carolina settled this area in the 1820's. Those of Scotch descent were for the most part members of the Associate Reformed Presbyterian Church. When they arrived they followed the old Scottish custom of forming 'societies' for performing basic religious activities while they searched for a minister.

The Rev. Henry Bryson is said to have been the first minister to conduct Baptisms and Communion services in the community. He or other ministers conducted services in a 'brush arbor' near the present church site. In July, 1830, Hopewell Church was organized and the first church building was erected. This building became the community's one-room school at a later date.

The first regular pastor was the Rev. Thomas Turner. The second, Rev. Henry Quigg, came shortly after completing seminary studies in 1854. Under his leadership a new church building was erected in 1856. This building, recently renovated, still stands today as the congregation's sanctuary.

In 1860, Hopewell Church hosted the annual conference of the General Synod of the Associate Reformed Presbyterian Church. Delegates attended from throughout the southeast.

The front section of the church was remodeled and expanded in the 1890's. The original two front doors were replaced with a single entrance and two rooms plus a vestibule were added.

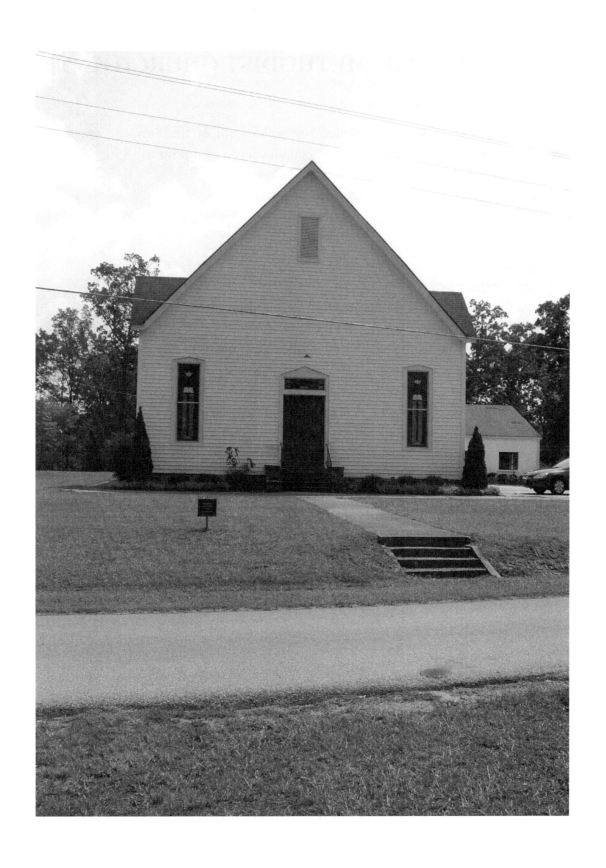

Hopewell A.R. Presbyterian Church   Circa 1856

RED OAK METHODIST CHURCH

Red Oak United Methodist Church is located one mile north of the Stewart community on Georgia Highway 36 in Newton County, GA. The church was erected prior to 1856.

A GHC marker at the site contains the following inscription:

Red Oak Church

Red Oak Church was established between 1803, when the Indians left this area, and late 1821, when Newton County was formed. The church grounds originally contained 4 acres, including the spring behind the church. The first building, between the present church and spring, was built of red oak logs, from which the church name is derived. Lorenzo Dow, on his mission to Georgia in 1803, is thought to have preached here and been instrumental in organizing the church. The present building is over 100 years old. Among the earliest graves in the cemetery in that of Major Lewis Hogg, Revolutionary Soldier, buried in September 1828.

Red Oak Methodist Church   Circa 1856

SALEM BAPTIST CHURCH

Salem Baptist Church is located on Salem Church Rd. in Rockdale County, GA.

Luke Roberson and Isaiah Parker who served as the church's first pastors established Salem Baptist Church on June 18, 1820. Charter members were James and Gracey Butler, George Fiedler, Elizabeth Welch and Temperance Lee. L.D. Echols donated the lot on which the church is situated in 1825. The present church building was erected in 1830. A gallery was added in 1844 for slaves who were church members.

Services at the church were held on an irregular basis during the Civil War because many members were serving in the Confederate army. After the war, membership declined and the church was disbanded, but it was shortly thereafter reorganized through the able assistance and guidance of Dr. J.M. Brittain, pastor of Covington Baptist Church.

Salem Baptist Church   Circa 1830

CLINTON METHODIST CHURCH

Clinton Methodist Church is located just west of Green Settlement Road on Dames Ferry Road in the community of Clinton, GA. in Jones County
.

A GHC marker at the site contains the following inscription:

Clinton Methodist Church

This is the first Methodist Church and the second church established in Jones County. Land was appropriated in 1810 and July 14, 1821 a deed to the Clinton Methodists was made effective. The church was "a frame house of good dimensions with substantial stone steps of native granite". A gallery for slaves was removed in 1897. The chandelier and brass wall brackets originally held kerosene lamps. This church was among the first to organize a foreign missionary society. Among the early pastors were Dr. Lovick Pierce and Rev. James Payne, 1836.

Clinton Methodist Church   **Circa 1825**

SAINT STEPHEN'S EPISCOPAL CHURCH

St. Stephen's Episcopal Church is located at 220 S. Wayne St. in the city of Milledgeville, GA. in Baldwin County. It was constructed in the Carpenter-Gothic style which was popular at the time.

It is said that because Episcopal leaders from the highest level down to the parish level had been strong supporters of secession, Union officers and soldiers who swept through the Southern states targeted Episcopal churches with a special vengeance. When they occupied Milledgeville, Union troops burned the church pews for firewood and stabled their horses in the church. Then they blew up the nearby armory and arsenal which demolished the church roof.

A GHC marker at the site has the following inscription:

St. Stephen's Episcopal Church

This Church was organized in 1841 through the efforts of Bishop Stephen Elliott. The church building was completed in 1843 and consecrated Dec. 10. The vestibule, annex and Gothic roof were added later. The hand made chancel furniture was given by an early parishioner, John Wilcox. Rev. Rufus Wright was probably the first Rector and J.M. Lotting and C.J. Paine the first Wardens. In 1864 the building was damaged when Federal troops dynamited the nearby arsenal. In 1909 a new organ was presented by George W. Perkins of New York who had heard that Sherman's troops stabled horses in the ruined building and further damaged its contents.

St. Stephens Episcopal Church   Circa 1843

MONTPELIER UNITED METHODIST CHURCH

Montpelier United Methodist Church is located east of the Oconee River on GA Highway 22 near its junction with GA Highway 24 in Baldwin County, GA.

During the 1790's problems with the Creek Indians and early settlers prompted the State of Georgia to build a chain of forts along the Oconee River. One of the forts was named Fort Fidius. Each of the forts was garrisoned by a troop of soldiers whose presence was intended to reduce the possibility of an all out Indian War. There were, however, attacks on isolated settlements and the nearest fort provided protection to nearby settlers.

A small community grew up near Ft. Fidius that became known as Montpelier. Montpelier Church was organized in 1794 and both Baptist and Methodist ministers preached there. In 1843 the church was moved on log rollers to the present site which had been donated by Col. Benjamin Hall. The church was then known as Montpelier Meeting House.

A GHC marker at the site has the following inscription:

Montpelier

This church is named Montpelier after Fort Montpelier of 1794 ½ mile below here down the Oconee. This fort and others were built during the Creek Indian troubles. Capt. Jonas Fouche was ordered to guard the GA frontier from the mouth of the Tugaloo to Fort Fidius on the Oconee. 200 militia cavalry & infantry raised under Gov. Telfair were placed under the command of Maj. Gaither, Federal commandant. A note on Fouche's map reads, "As it is 40 mi. from Fort Twiggs to Mount Pelah where Maj. Gaither lies in garrison, it is recommended that a public station might be created by the Government (at Cedar Shoals)."

Montpelier Methodist Church   Circa 1840

CHRIST EPISCOPAL CHURCH

Christ Episcopal Church is located on Walnut Street in the city of Macon, GA in Bibb County. This church is often referred to as the `Mother Church of the Diocese of Atlanta' and claims to be the oldest congregation of any denomination in Macon. There is a plaque affixed to the church that states the church was built in 1851.

A GHC marker at the site contains the following inscription:

Christ Church Episcopal

The Reverend Lot Jones, while on a missionary tour of Georgia, founded Christ Episcopal Church on March 5, 1825. It was the first congregation organized in Macon. On December 26, 1826, the Georgia General Assembly enacted, "that Christopher B. Strong, Edward D. Tracy, Albert G. Clopton, Addison Mandell and Reuben Burroughs are hereby declared to be a body corporate, by the name and style of the Protestant Episcopal Church in the town of Macon and the County of Bibb." Under the leadership of the Reverend Seneca G. Bragg, the first church building was erected in 1834.

The Reverend Joseph A. Shanklin was rector when this Gothic structure was erected. On Sunday, May 2, 1852, it was consecrated by the Right Reverend Stephen Elliott, the first bishop of Georgia. James B. Ayers was the master builder. The original church bell was given to the Confederate Government in 1863 and in 1868 a new bell was presented to the church by A.A. Roff, a member. The bell bears the inscription: "On earth peace, good will to men."

Sidney Lanier, poet, was married to Miss Mary Day in Christ Church on December 19, 1867.

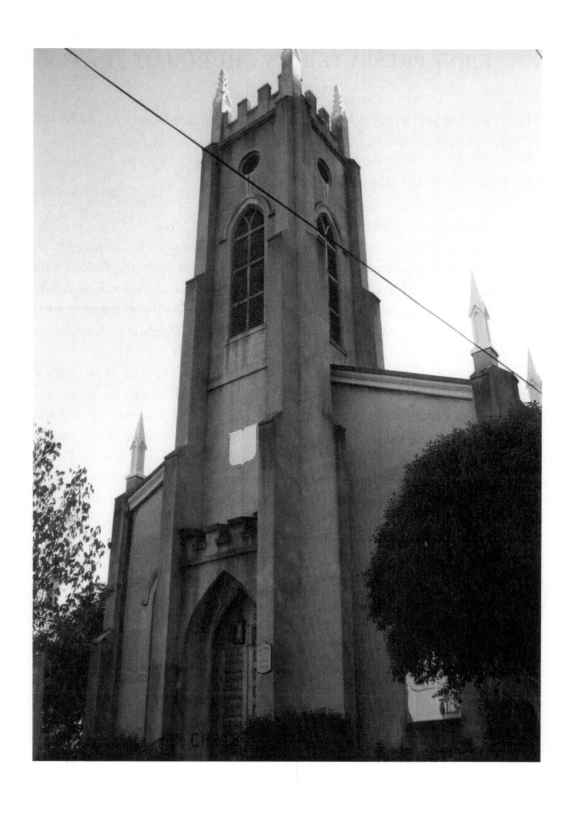

Christ Episcopal Church   Circa 1851

FIRST PRESBYTERIAN CHURCH OF MACON

The First Presbyterian Church is located on the corner of First Street and Mulberry Street in the city of Macon, GA in Bibb County.

A GHC marker at the site contains the following inscription:

The First Presbyterian Church

Organized as the First Presbyterian Church of Macon on June 18, 1826, by the Rev. Benjamin Guildersleeve and the Rev. Joseph C. Stiles, the church dedicated this house of worship, its third on September 19, 1858, at the close of the ministry of the Rev. Robert L. Breck. Mr. Stiles was the first Pastor; Matthew Robertson and Samuel B. Hunter, ordained October 14, 1827, the first elders.

This church was host for the formation of the Synod of Georgia in 1844 with Dr. Thomas Goulding, founder and first president of Columbia Seminary as moderator. His son, the Rev. Francis R. Goulding, author of The Young Marooners, served here in the 60's by preaching to the Negro members who withdrew to form Washington Avenue Presbyterian Church in 1866. This is the Mother Church also of Tatnall Square (1887), Vinevill (1904) and East Macon (1906).

It was the younger Goulding who took over the city-wide Thanksgiving service commanded here by the Union General Wilson at the close of the War Between the States because the pastor, the Rev. David Willis, was overcome by the mockery of the occasion. Goulding's service consisted of reading Psalm 137 "..For they that carried us away captive required of us a song."

In the church vestibule is a plaque honoring Sidney Lanier, who was a member here.

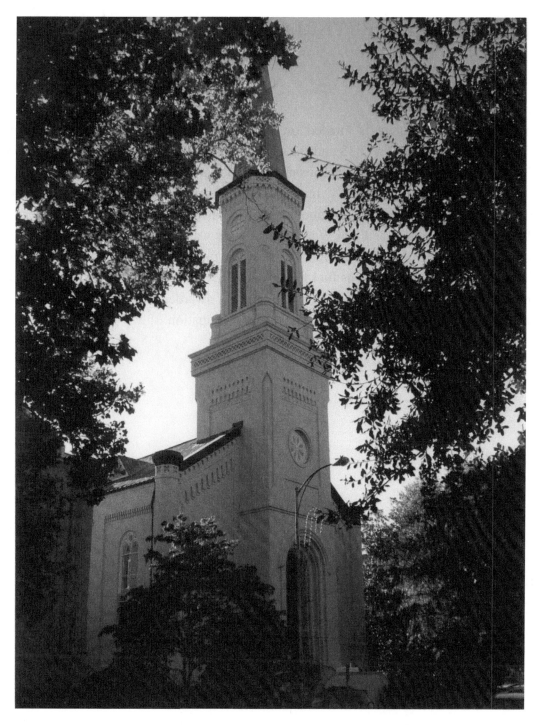

First Presbyterian Church of Macon   Circa 1858

FIRST PRESBYTERIAN CHURCH OF MARIETTA

The First Presbyterian Church is located on Church Street in the city of Marietta in Cobb County, GA. It was organized in 1835 and the first church building, a small frame structure, was built in 1839. It was replaced by the present sanctuary, which was completed in 1854.

Cadets from nearby Georgia Military Institute, which was established in Marietta in 1851, frequently attended services in the new sanctuary. Most of these young men would later serve in the Confederate army. During the Civil War, the sanctuary was used as a hospital by Union forces that occupied Marietta in 1864. The church was severely damaged by the occupying troops who, it was claimed, burned church pews as fuel for cooking, spat tobacco juice on the walls and floors and destroyed church windows. In 1915, the church was awarded three thousand dollars by the U.S. Court of Claims for damages sustained during the occupation.

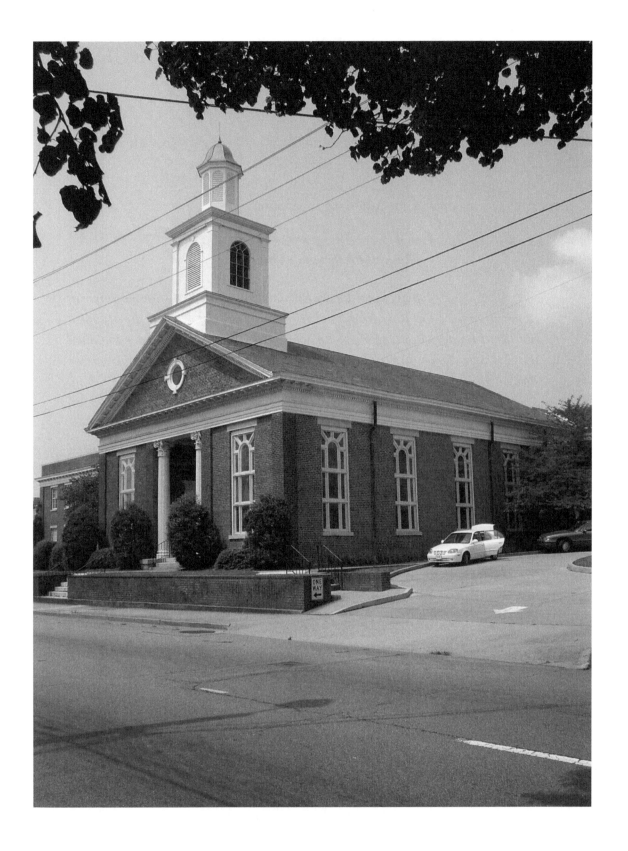

First Presbyterian Church of Marietta   Circa 1854

ROSWELL PRESBYTERIAN CHURCH

Roswell Presbyterian Church is located on Mimosa Blvd. in the city of Roswell in Fulton County, GA.

A GHC marker at the site contains the following inscription:

Roswell Presbyterian Church

In 1859, 15 Presbyterian men and women, "members of the colony" of Roswell, invited the Rev. Nathaniel A. Pratt, D.D., of Darien, to organize the first Presbyterian church of Roswell. These charter members included the Bulloch, Dunwoody, Hand, King, Smith, Pratt families, and Misses Elizabeth and Helen Magill, Susan Elliott and Sarah Gould. John Dunwoody, Sr. Barrington King, and Archibald Smith were elected elders. Dr. Pratt, the first pastor, served until his death, 40 years later. The Rev. Henry Barrington Pratt, whose Spanish translation of the Bible is used today, went from this church as a missionary to Columbia in 1856; Dr. Butler to Brazil in 1883. The early membership included several Negro slaves. Of these, Charles Pratt and John Hall became missionaries to Africa.

In July, 1864, the advance guard of Gen. Garrard's Cavalry Corps commandeered this church for a hospital, removing the furnishings. Except the pipe organ, these were returned intact after the war. The silver communion service in use today was hidden by Miss Fannie Whitmire in a barrel at her home until the end of the war.

Roswell Presbyterian Church   Circa 1860

UTOY PRIMITIVE BAPTIST CHURCH

Utoy Church is located at the corner of Venetian Drive and Cahaba Drive in the city of Atlanta, GA in Fulton County. It was the oldest Baptist Church in present day Fulton County and was built circa 1828. It is now the Temple of Christ Pentecostal Church. During the Battle of Atlanta this church was used as a Confederate hospital and approximately 25 Confederate soldiers, casualties of the battle of Utoy Creek, are buried in the church cemetery.

A GHC marker at the site has the following inscription:

Historic Utoy Church

Utoy Primitive Baptist Church, the oldest Baptist Church in present Fulton County, was constituted August 15, 1824, in a log house just west of here. The church was moved to the present location in the summer of 1828.

In 1864 the church was used as a Confederate hospital. July 22, Col. James S. Boynton, 30th Georgia, was wounded and brought to Utoy Church for medical care. Boynton later became President of the Georgia Senate and on March 5, 1883, the day after the death of Governor Alexander H. Stephens, he became Governor of Georgia to serve until a special election could be held.

In the cemetery of Utoy Church lies buried Dr. Joshua Gilbert, Atlanta's first doctor. Born in 1815 in South Carolina, Dr. Gilbert was graduated from old Augusta Medical College in 1845 and came to Atlanta. At that time Atlanta was called Marthasville and was located in DeKalb County. Here he practiced medicine until his death in 1889.

Utoy Church   Circa 1828

VAN WERT METHODIST CHURCH

Van Wert Methodist Church is located on Garner St. in the Van Wert community approximately one mile south of the city of Rockmart, GA. in Polk County. The church was organized in 1846 and the present building was erected that year. The Campbell family donated the land for the church. During Sherman's March toward Atlanta, the church and church grounds were occupied by Union troops of Gen. Dodge's 16th Army Corps.

In 1882 the Rockmart First Methodist Church was formed by former members of Van Wert Methodist church. The church steadily declined in membership and by 1948 the building had deteriorated to the point that the roof caved in and the church steeple lay on the church floor. Church members and the Campbell family began the renovation process, but services were sporadic from 1950-1974. In 1980 services were discontinued and the building became the property of the Polk County Historical Society.

The Rev. Sam P. Jones, who later became an internationally renowned evangelist, was appointed pastor of Van Wert Methodist Church in 1872.

VanWert Methodist Church   Circa 1846

FIRST PRESBYTERIAN CHURCH OF CARTERSVILLE

The First Presbyterian Church of Cartersville is located at 183 W. Main St. in the city of Cartersville, GA. in Bartow County. It was established in 1843 and was then called Friendship Presbyterian Church. The church was at first situated near the Etowah River, but in 1853 the congregation moved to the present location. The new building was designed with a balcony to accommodate slaves. In 1887 the name was changed to the First Presbyterian Church of Cartersville.

During Sherman's March toward Atlanta in the Civil War, Union troops occupied the church and used it as a blacksmith shop. During the occupation of the city, Union forces demolished the First Baptist Church and used the bricks to construct their quarters and to erect chimneys for their tents. The Baptist congregation was invited to use the First Presbyterian Church for their services until they were able to construct a new sanctuary in 1869.

The masonry façade and present bell towers were added at a later date

First Presbyterian Church of Cartersville   **Circa 1853**

PINE LOG UNITED METHODIST CHURCH

Pine Log United Methodist Church is located on Pine Log Rd. near US Hwy 411 in northern Bartow County, GA. It was constructed in the 1840's.

A church marker at the site contains the following inscription:

Historic Pine Log Methodist Church

250' west of this marker stands Historic Pine Log Methodist Church, Cemetery, Tabernacle and Camp Grounds, established in 1834. The oldest Church in continuous use in Cass/Bartow County. This Church area is on the National Register for Historic District.

This sign erected by the Pine Log Historical Society and the Men's Club of historic Pine Log Methodist Church, dedicated to the Glory of God and the Early Settlers of Pine Log Georgia.

A marble marker affixed to the church has the following inscription:

On this site, Aug. 31, 1886 Reverend J.N. Sullivan prayed this prayer:
"Lord, if it takes it to move the hearts of these people, shake the grounds on which this old building stands."
Before the conclusion of Rev. Sullivan's prayer, the grounds were violently shaken by a sudden earthquake.
"The effectual fervent prayer of a righteous man availeth much." James 5:16

Pine Log Methodist Church   Circa 1845

LIBERTY CUMBERLAND PRESBYTERIAN CHURCH

Liberty Cumberland Presbyterian Church is located three miles west of the city of Calhoun, GA. at 1115 Liberty Church Rd. in Gordon County. This church is also known historically as White Church. The church was organized in 1853 by the Rev. S.H. Henry. In 1860 the present building was erected on a two acre tract.

While Sherman's March toward Atlanta was taking place during the Civil War, the area was occupied by Union troops and the church was used as a hospital. Local tradition holds that Union troops used church literature, hymnals, and pews as firewood while camped on church grounds.

Liberty Cumberland Presbyterian Church   Circa 1860

ST. PAUL CME CHURCH

St. Paul CME Church is located on East 6th Ave. in the City of Rome in Floyd County, GA. This church was built originally for the Methodist congregation of Rome on land given to the church by Col. Daniel R. Mitchell, one of the city's founders.

Originally constructed of brick in the 1840's, this building, which once housed the First Methodist congregation, now is the home of St. Paul CME Church. It is at present covered with stucco to protect and preserve the brick walls. Union troops occupied Rome during the Civil War and used this church as a stable for their horses.

St. Paul CME Church   Circa 1845

THE FIRST PRESBYTERIAN CHURCH OF ROME

The First Presbyterian Church of Rome is located on East Third Ave. in the city of Rome in Floyd County, GA.

In 1833 a Presbyterian church was established in the small community of Livingston under the leadership of the Rev. John Wilson and was called Livingston Church. By 1845 the congregation had moved to Rome and in 1854 the present church was constructed, built with bricks made on the Bailey farm on the Coosa River below Rome.

During the Civil War the Union army occupied Rome and requisitioned the church as a food warehouse during Sherman's campaign in Georgia. During this period the church pews were removed and were used to build a bridge over the river and to provide horse stalls for the Union Cavalry.

The war caused great hardship and the congregation became scattered and disorganized and declined to some fifty members, but shortly after the war ended the membership began growing again and by 1885 there were some 300 active church members on the church role.

It was in this church that Woodrow Wilson, a young attorney then practicing law in Atlanta, met Ellen Louise Axson, who later became his wife. Her father, Samuel Axson, was pastor of the church from 1866 through 1883. When Mrs. Wilson died in the White House in 1914, President Wilson brought her body back to Rome and the funeral was held in this church.

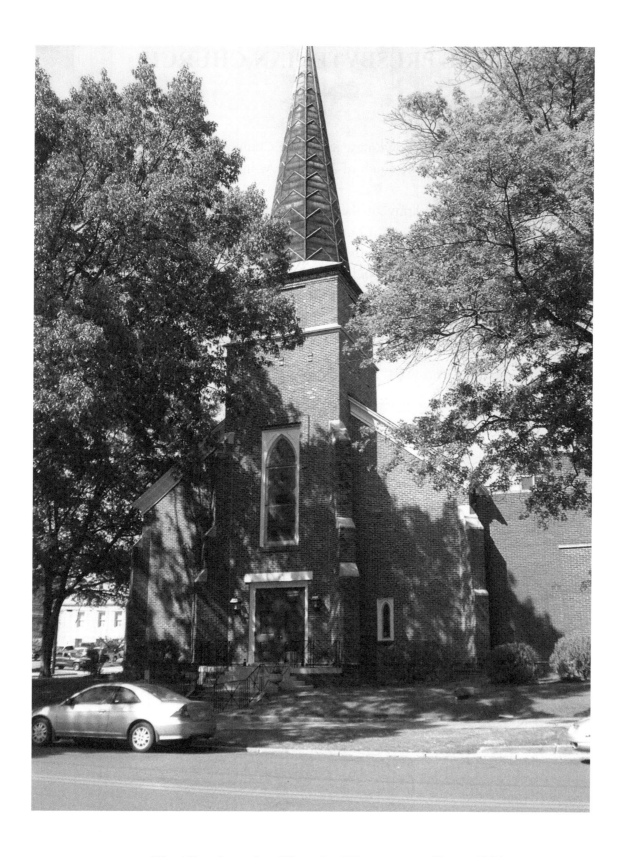

First Presbyterian Church of Rome   **Circa 1854**

ALPINE PRESBYTERIAN CHURCH

The Alpine Presbyterian Church, known now as Alpine Community Church, is located on GA Highway 337 approximately one mile south of Menlo, GA. in Walker County. The church was built in 1853.

In September, 1863, the Union Army of the Cumberland began moving toward Georgia by crossing Sand Mountain and heading east. Confederate generals Joseph Wheeler, Nathan Bedford Forrest and John A. Wharton met at Alpine Church to make plans for resisting the Union advance. There is a painting entitled *'Prelude to Chickamauga'* by John White depicting these three Confederate army leaders meeting at Alpine Church.

After the Battle of Chickamauga, the church pews were utilized as beds to accommodate Confederate wounded and the church building was used as a Confederate hospital.

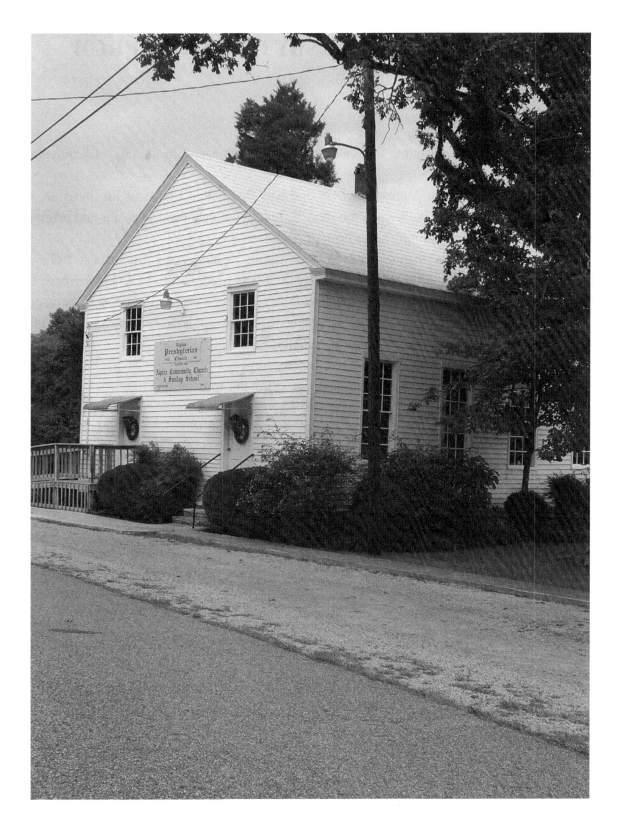

Alpine Presbyterian Church   Circa 1853

LAFAYETTE PRESBYTERIAN CHURCH

The LaFayette Presbyterian Church is located on North Main Street in the city of LaFayette in Walker County, GA.

The church was organized on August 12, 1836 and was first called Ebenezer Presbyterian. The present sanctuary was built in 1848 when the Rev. William H. Johnston was pastor and originally included a slave gallery that has long since been removed.

In June of 1864, during Sherman's march toward Atlanta, a battle was fought near LaFayette resulting in many casualties. After the battle, the church was used as a field hospital where both Confederate and Union soldiers were treated. Boards were placed across the pews to be used as operating tables. Many soldiers who died as a result of their wounds were placed outside in the churchyard to await eventual burial in the local cemetery.

A marble marker affixed to the church contains the following inscription:

Presbyterian Church

Erected 1848

Used as a hospital for both Confederate and Union forces after the Battle of LaFayette.

June 24, 1864

LaFayette Presbyterian Church   **Circa 1848**

OLD STONE PRESBYTERIAN CHURCH

Old Stone Presbyterian Church is located on GA. Highway 2 just east of the juncture with US Highway 41 in Catoosa County, GA. It was constructed using large blocks of sandstone from a quarry located near Calhoun's Mill. The building took two years to complete at a cost of $1,600.

A GHC marker at the site has the following inscription:

Old Stone Presbyterian Church Wartime Hospital

This church, organized September 2, 1837, before the Cherokee Indians were removed from this area, was the first church organized by white settlers in the bounds of the present Catoosa County, according to available records. The organizers were a group Scotch Irish Presbyterians from Tennessee or the Carolinas and the Charter Members were: Robert Magill, James H. McSpadden, Robert C. Cain, Sara Black, Alfred McSpadden, Fanny Magill, Susan McSpadden, Winifred Cain, Margaret Cain and Nancy Tipton. This building of sandstone quarried nearby, was erected in 1850 and following the Battle of Ringgold, November 27, 1863, was used as a hospital. Blood stains are still visible on the floor. It remained a Presbyterian Church until about 1920 when it was sold to a Methodist congregation which maintained it for some years. It then passed into private hands and to save it from destruction a group of descendents of the early members raised a fund and purchased it, deeding it to a board of trustees to be used for religious purposes. In recent years it has been used by various denominations.

A private marker at the site states, in part, the following:

"This building commonly called 'The Old Stone Church' began construction in the Summer of 1850..."
"This structure is erected from stone quarried from the Stubblefield farm and from the base of White Oak Mountain. Timber was procured from dense forests in the area. The total cost is said to be only $1,600.00 and construction took two years..."
"It is reported that the benches were placed facing each other and used for fodder troughs for the Union Army's horses. These benches show evidence of indentations of the horses' teeth..."

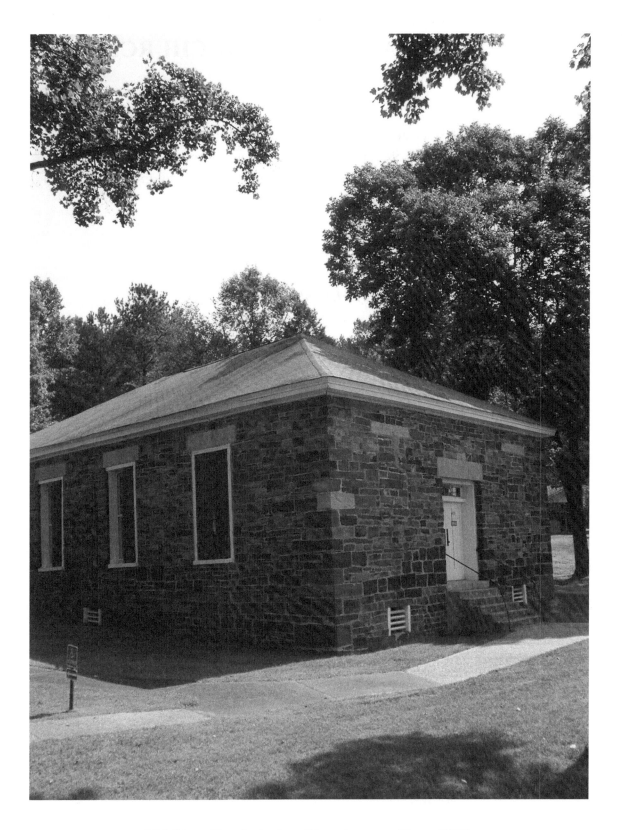

Old Stone Presbyterian Church   Circa 1850

CARTECAY METHODIST CHURCH

Cartecay Methodist Church is located on GA. Highway 52 in Gilmer County, GA.

The present building, erected in 1859, remains, in style and arrangement, as originally built. During the War Between the States, the building was guarded at night by groups of men to protect it from Union sympathizers who roamed the countryside.

A GHC marker at the site contains the following inscription:

Cartecay Methodist Church

This church, Cartecay Methodist (South), was organized and a building erected in August 1834 on the property of Lewis D. Ellington. The first preacher was William Ellington, ordained in 1805 by Bishop Asbury. The first Sunday School was organized April 20, 1851 and has operated continuously.

Among the early preachers were: Rev. Bethel Quillian, Rev. John B. Robeson, Rev. A.J. Hughes, Rev. A.J. Hutchinson, Rev. C.M. Ledbetter, Rev. John W. Quillian, Rev. M.L. Underwood, Rev. C.A. Jamison, Dr. John Watkins, Rev. J.O. Butler, Rev. A.D. Echols, Rev. Walter B. Dillard, Rev. R.B.O. England, Rev. C.W. Griner, Rev. W.L. Singleton, Rev. J.N. Myers, Rev. W.C. Hunnicutt, Rev. John B. Pettit. As a young man, Bishop Warren Candler preached here.

Cartecay Methodist Church   Circa 1859

GRACE EPISCOPAL CHURCH

Grace Episcopal Church is located on Green Street in the city of Clarkesville in Habersham County, GA. It is said to be the oldest virtually unchanged Episcopal Church building in Georgia. It was built by Jarvis Van Buren, a relative of President Martin Van Buren. The church windows for the most part are original, hand-blown glass panes and the organ, built in 1845, is reported to be the oldest working pipe organ in the state.

Clarkesville was founded in 1823 on lands ceded by treaty with the Cherokee. Hotels and boarding houses were built in short order to accommodate the well-to-do families of coastal Georgia and South Carolina who wished to escape the fevers and intense heat of summer. Clarkesville became one of the first major mountain resorts in north Georgia.

The Episcopal faith had grown so rapidly that the Bishop of the Diocese of South Carolina could no longer continue to serve the two states. Accordingly, in May of 1840, the 18th Annual Convention of the Diocese of Savannah was held in Clarkesville for the purpose of electing the first Bishop for the Diocese. Because Grace Episcopal Church was still under construction, the convention was held in the Methodist Church and the Rev. Stephen Elliott, Jr. was elected Bishop.

A local tradition recounts that during the last year of the Civil War, town residents hid their horses in the church to prevent their seizure by Union foragers. The end of the Civil War brought years of hardship to Grace Episcopal. Many families from the coastal region were now destitute and most did not return to Clarkesville. A few sold their coastal property and permanently settled in their former summer residences.

A GHC marker at the site has the following inscription:

Grace Protestant Episcopal Church

The first Episcopal service in Clarkesville was held Oct. 28, 1838, by the Rev. Mr. Ezra B. Kellogg, sent from N.Y. to the Diocese of Georgia as a missionary to this section. On Dec. 12, 1838, at his home, Grace Church was organized for three local Episcopal families and the many coastal families who spent their summers here. On April 15, 1839, this, the sixth Episcopal Church in the State, was admitted to the Diocese. On June 7, 1839, this square acre lot was purchased from John Brannon for $100. For the first year services were held in the Methodist Church and Clarkesville Academy.

In 1841, the Rev. J.B. Gallagher succeeded as Rector. Under his guidance, this building, begun in 1839, was completed in 1842. It was consecrated Oct. 6, 1842, by the Rt. Rev. Stephen Elliott, Jr., (first) Bishop of Georgia, who reported it as "A very neat wooden building, with tower and bell, prettily located and an ornament to the village."

Among prominent early members were: Richard W. Habersham, Sr., John R. Matthews. Wardens: Alexander Irwin, Benjamin F. Patton, George D. Phillips, John R. Sanford, Samuel A. Wales, John S. Dobbins, Dr. Phineas M. Kallock, Jacob Waldberg. Vestrymen: Richard W. Habersham, Jr., George B. Jessup, Lay delegates to the Convention that admitted this Church to the Diocese.

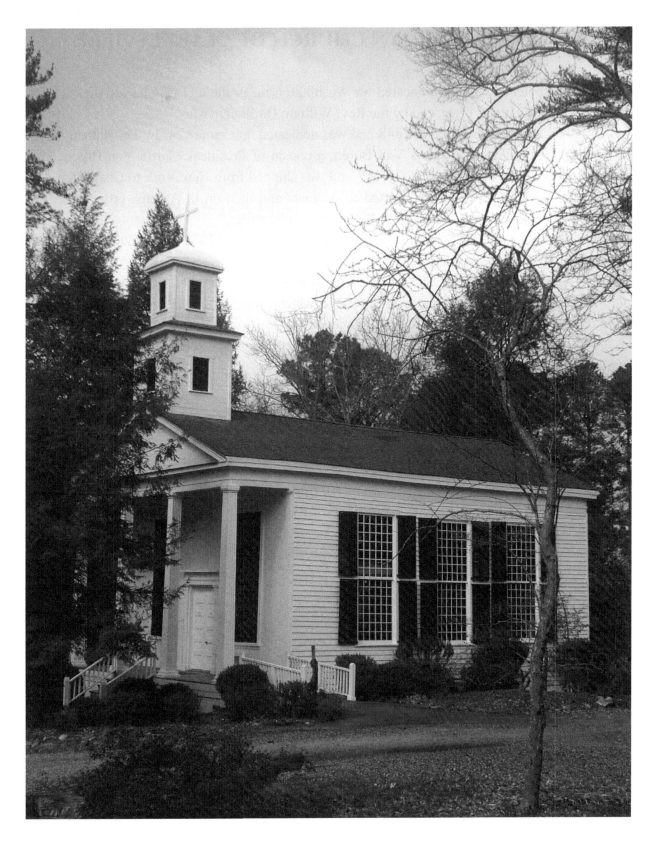

Grace Episcopal Church   **Circa 1839**

FIRST PRESBYTERIAN CHURCH OF CLARKESVILLE

The First Presbyterian Church is located on Washington St. in the city of Clarkesville, GA. in Habersham County. It was organized by the Rev. William Quillian in May, 1832.

The church building was erected in 1848 and was dedicated that same year by Dr. Nathan Hoyt. The designer and builder was Jarvis Van Buren, a cousin of President Martin Van Buren. The church bell was cast in a foundry in Troy, NY and was shipped from New York to Charleston, SC by sea. From Charleston it was transported to Augusta and then on to Athens. From Athens a wagon driver was hired to haul the 710 lb. Bell on to Clarkesville.

The church still has in use a pulpit bible that was published in 1822 and remains a beloved heirloom from the congregation's earliest period.

An early pastor of the church, Dr. R.C. Ketchem, was selected as one of the two Habersham County citizens to sign the Ordinance of Secession which prepared the way for Georgia to leave the Union and join the Confederate States of America

In 1907 the church was moved from its original site to its present location. The building was extensively renovated and stabilized in 1976.

Some of the church's early pastors included the following:

William Quillian	Founding Pastor
Stanhope Erwin	1832-1838
C. Bradshaw	1838-1844
Homer Hendee	1844-1845
R.C. Ketchum	1848-1866

First Presbyterian Church of Clarkesville   **Circa 1848**

COLLINSWORTH METHODIST CHURCH

Collinsworth Methodist Church is located on Po Biddy Rd. in Talbot County, GA.

A small group of Methodists met to form a Methodist Society in the home of George Menifee in the late 1820's. In 1830, a Methodist church was organized by members of this Society and the first church building to be erected was a log cabin. In 1834 this structure was replaced by the present building which was called Collinsworth Chapel in honor of Rev. John Collinsworth, a former pastor. This building was dedicated in 1859 by Rev. Lovick Pierce.

A number of former Confederate soldiers who were members of the Collinsworth congregation are buried in the church cemetery.

Collinsworth Methodist Church   Circa 1834

TALBOTTON UNITED METHODIST CHURCH

Talbotton United Methodist Church is located on U.S. 80 north of College St. in the city of Talbotton, GA. in Talbot County.

A South Georgia (Methodist) Conference marker at the site contains the following inscription:

Talbotton United Methodist

As Methodism moved across Georgia, in 1830 Jessie Sinclair and Henry W. Hilliard were sent by the South Carolina Methodist Conference to the Flint River Mission of which Talbot County was a part. In 1831 this circuit became a part of the newly formed Georgia Conference and by 1834 Talbotton became a separate Charge.

Upon the incorporation of Talbotton on 20 December 1828 a lot was set aside for a Methodist Church and deeded to it on 25 June 1831. Soon a substantial wooden church was erected. In 1857 this building was replaced by the present handmade brick church constructed by Miranda Fort.

Among the oldest brick churches of the South Georgia Conference, it is an outstanding example of Greek Revival temple Architecture.

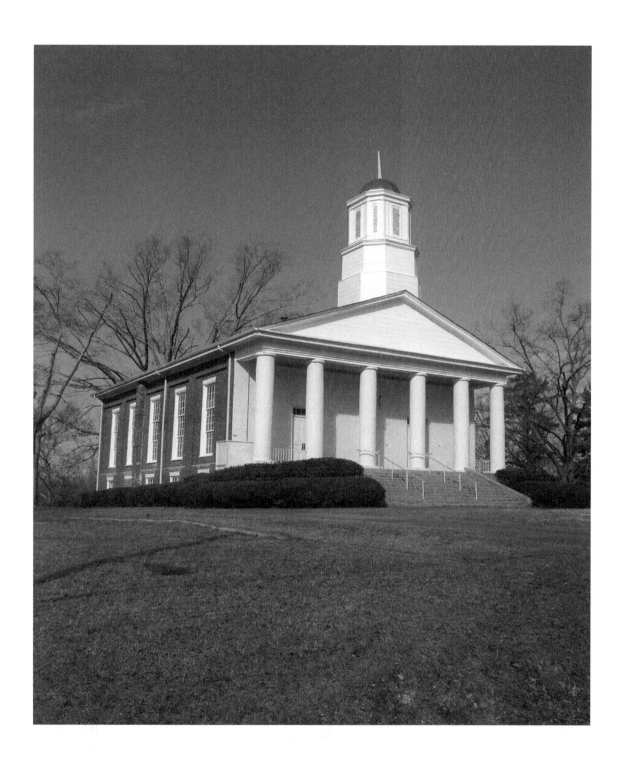

Talbotton Methodist Church   Circa 1857

ZION EPISCOPAL CHURCH

Zion Episcopal Church is located on GA Highway 41 in the city of Talbotton, GA. in Talbot County. The building was erected in 1848 when this area of Georgia was sparsely settled. It is presently being renovated by several private individuals in anticipation of receiving new members.

A GHC marker at the site bears the following inscription:

Zion Episcopal Church

The edifice has been spared modernization and is a perfect replica of a typical English rural parish of the Tudor-Gothic period.

The altar, communion rail, lectern-pulpit, and prayer desk are handmade of native walnut. The entire structure is put together with wooden pegs and handmade iron nails. The pipe organ, installed in 1850, and in continuous use since that time, is a Pilcher and still is operated by hand pump.

The choir loft at the east end of the structure opposite the sanctuary, above the narthex, is flanked on each side by a gallery, where slaves worshipped prior to the conflict which many believed temporarily destroyed Southern culture.

Zion Church had its incipience from the missionary zeal of the Rev. Richard Johnson and the financial assistance of South Carolina rice planters.

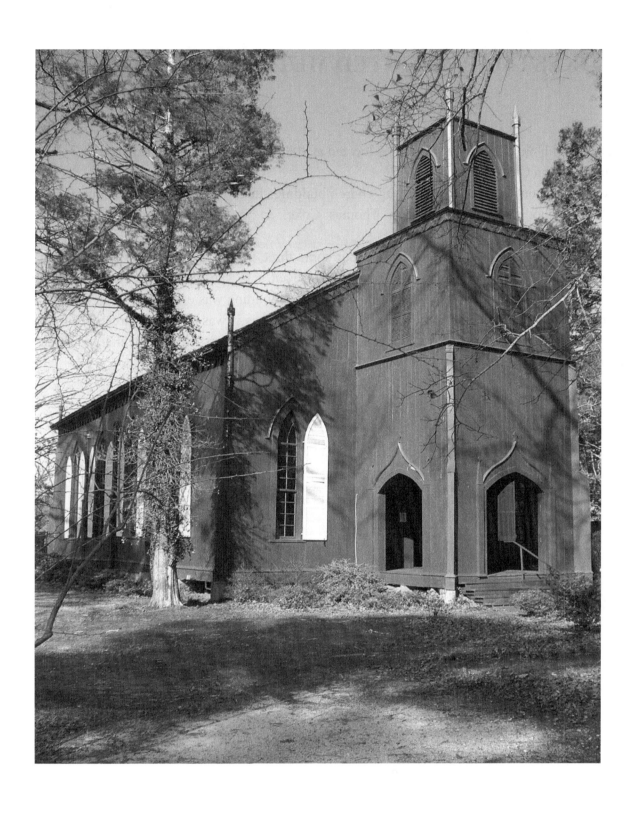

Zion Episcopal Church   Circa 1848

COKES CHAPEL UNITED METHODIST CHURCH

Cokes Chapel United Methodist Church is located at 4096 Lower Fayetteville Rd. in Sharpsburg, GA in Coweta County.

Cokes Chapel is one of the oldest existing church buildings in Coweta County. The church was named for Methodist Episcopal Bishop Thomas Coke, an important figure in establishing Methodism in America.

The congregation initially met in a Brush Arbor some three miles west of the present location before occupying a log cabin erected at the present seven acre site which was deeded to the church trustees for twenty-five dollars. In 1850 the present building was erected by R.D. Cole for a total cost of $1,100.00. The church building remains much as it was when constructed. In the cemetery next to the church are buried Confederate and Union soldiers and both white and black church members.

Cokes Chapel Methodist Church   Circa 1850

WHITESVILLE METHODIST CHURCH

Whitesville Methodist Church is located on Pine Lake Rd. in Whitesville, GA. in Harris County.

A HCC historical marker at the site contains the following inscription:

Whitesville Methodist Episcopal Church, South

The Methodist church in Whitesville had its origins about 1828 in meetings held at the home of Reuben Mobley. The First Methodist Church was founded in the early 1830s and by 1837 the decision was made to erect a church for the growing congregation on land donated by a trustee. The first church was used until 1854 when the current building was completed. This was the early church of Rev. William Jackson Callahan, an 1891 Emory graduate who was a missionary in Japan. Rev. Charles L. Allen, later pastor of Grace Methodist Church in Atlanta and well-known author, preached his first sermon here.

The Whitesville Methodist Church has been actively in use as a Methodist church since its dedication.

Whitesville Methodist Church   Circa 1854

FRANKLIN METHODIST CHURCH

Franklin Methodist Church is located on Main St., in the city of Franklin in Heard County, GA.

A GHC marker at the site has the following inscription:

Franklin Methodist Church

This, the Franklin Methodist Church, erected in 1831, is one of the earliest permanent church buildings in this area. Constructed of 12x12 hand-hewn pine beams, the church has been extensively remodeled through the years except the steeple, which stands as first built. The slave balcony originally in this church, unlike most, was at the front behind the pulpit. Early members have told of Indians worshiping in this building in the days when the Indian population of this section was large. Among the leaders of this church 100 years ago were the Lane, Daniel, Hammond, McCutchen and Lipford families.

Franklin Methodist Church   Circa 1831

COVENANT PRESBYTERIAN CHURCH

Covenant Presbyterian Church is located at 118 Church St. in the city of LaGrange, GA. in Troup County. The church was erected in 1844 and is the original home of the First Presbyterian Church in LaGrange. It is the oldest nonresidential structure in the city. During the Civil War from 1863-1865 the church was used as a Confederate hospital.

The Rev. James Woodrow, a Presbyterian minister and the uncle of future President Woodrow Wilson, was tried for heresy in this building. In recent years the building has housed several other Christian denominations and has served as a funeral home.

Covenant Presbyterian Church   Circa 1844

FIRST BAPTIST CHURCH OF COLUMBUS

The First Baptist Church of Columbus is located at 212 12th St. in the City of Columbus in Muscogee County, GA.

A HCC marker at the site has the following inscription:

First Baptist Church

On February 14, 1829, twelve persons met and organized under the name of Ephesus Baptist Church of Columbus. The northern half of this block had been designated to be used for religious purposes in the state survey of 1828, and a small meeting house was built for the church on this site in 1830. This was replaced by a larger frame structure in 1840, the same year the General Assembly of Georgia granted a charter to the Baptist Church of Columbus. The name was changed to First Baptist Church of Columbus, Georgia, in 1896. The present sanctuary was constructed in 1859. The Doric columns and wings were added in this century.

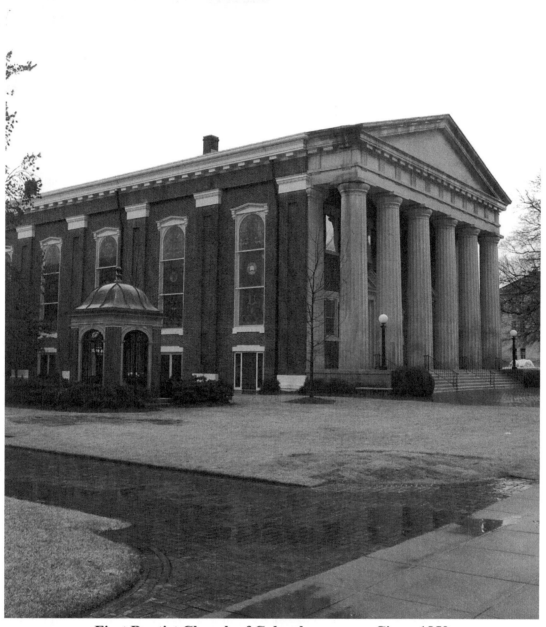

First Baptist Church of Columbus   Circa 1859

FIRST PRESBYTERIAN CHURCH OF COLUMBUS

The First Presbyterian Church of Columbus is located at 1100 First Ave. in the city of Columbus, GA. in Muscogee County.

An HCC marker at the site contains the following inscription:

First Presbyterian Church

Side 1

The Presbyterians were granted one of the original church lots in the 1828 Columbus plan. It was on the north side of Chapel St. between Second and Third Avenues. The fourteen charter members, received in 1830, were: Edward Featherston, William Root, James S. Norman, Richard T. Marks, David Dean, Thomas B. McCreary, John Johnson, Mrs. Jane L. Marks, Mrs. Leah J. Norman, Mrs. Harriet A. Root, Mrs. Miriam Dean, Mrs. Sarah DeGraffenried, Mrs. Eliza Bullock, Miss Rebecca Featherston. In 1831 the congregation was granted a lot at the northeast corner of Second Ave. and Tenth St., where services were held for thirty years. The move to Eleventh St. and First Ave. came in 1862.

Side 2

The First Presbyterian Church building on the northeast corner of Eleventh St. and First Ave. was dedicated in 1862. In 1891 the sanctuary was severely damaged by fire. It reopened for services in 1893. After the fire, the "city" clock was placed in the bell tower. The design of the building is Romanesque. Wings were constructed in 1925 and a free-standing chapel in 1952. Renovations were made in 1969 and an addition in 1974. The General Assembly of the Presbyterian Church, U.S. was hosted by First Church in 1982, when the vote to reunite the U.S. and U.S.A. churches was taken. Placed on the National Register of Historic Places in 1980.

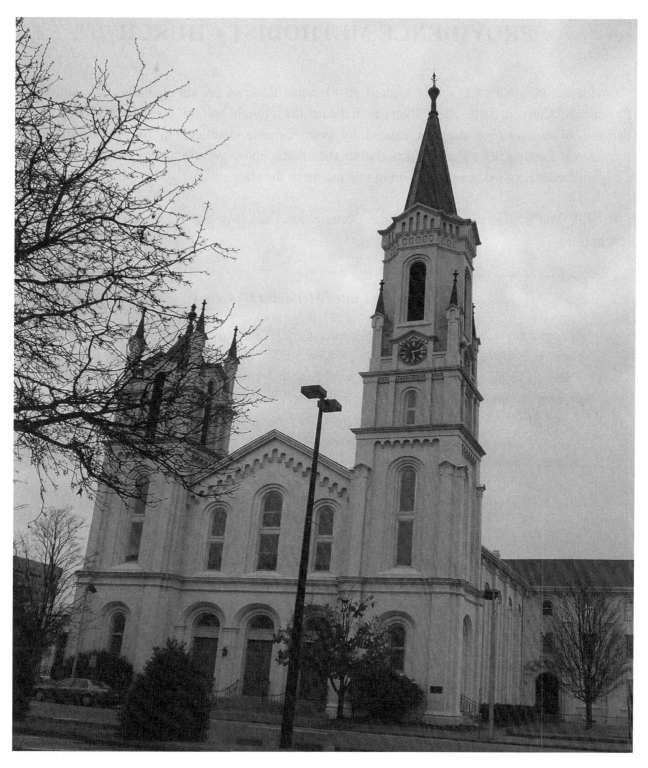

First Presbyterian Church of Columbus   Circa 1862

PROVIDENCE METHODIST CHURCH

Providence Methodist Church is located on Florence Road in Stewart County, GA. adjoining Providence Canyon State Park. Records indicate the church had to be moved around 1860 because of encroaching canyons caused by poor farming practices in the immediate area. Providence Canyon State Park is named after the church and is referred to as "The Little Grand Canyon" because of the severe erosion in this region of the state.

An HCC and Stewart County Historical Commission marker at the site contains the following inscription:

Providence United Methodist Church

Providence Church, when first organized, 1832-33, was a log building on the south side of the road. Two acres were donated by David Lowe for a church and school (Providence Academy). This land is now between two of the canyons. The present building was built in 1859, on the north side of the old Lumpkin-Florence Road. Many Stewart County pioneer families are buried in the cemetery. Charter members were Goodes, Lowes, Worthingtons, Perkins, Kirkpatricks, Seays, Pitts, Adams, Shermans, and Pattersons.

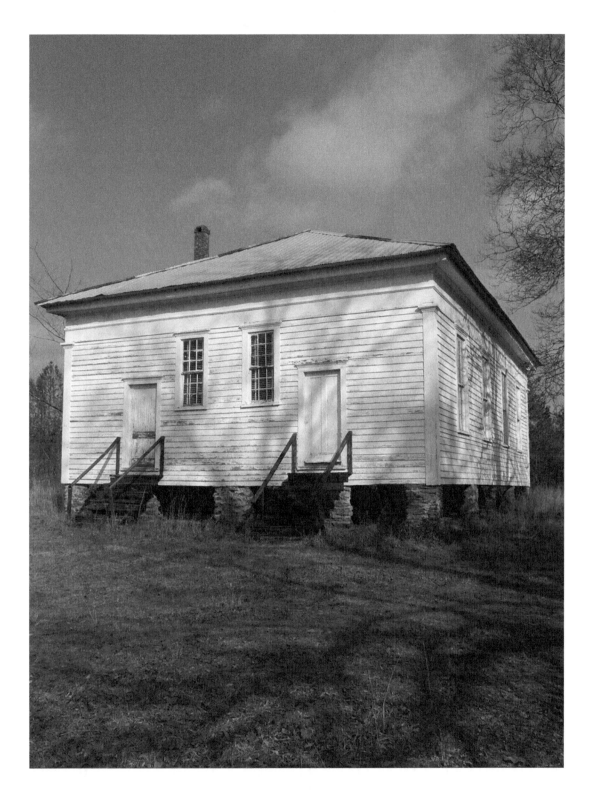

Providence Methodist Church   Circa 1859

PROVIDENCE CHAPEL CHRISTIAN CHURCH

Providence Chapel is located on old US Highway 280 north of Richland at Red Hill in Stewart County, GA. It is said the ceiling, flooring and framing of the church still show the hand plane marks made during its construction.

A GHC marker at the site has the following inscription:

Providence Chapel

The first Christian Church in Georgia was constituted at this site in 1857. Services were held in the 1830's by Rev. George Lynch Smith, first under a brush arbor and later in a log schoolhouse. This building, then two-story, was erected in 1857 under the pastorate of Rev. Smith's son, Dr. Jubilee Smith, pastor until 1895. The second story was used by the Smith Lodge No. 233 Masons from its organization in 1858. First officers were Dr. Smith, Jonathon Bridges, J.B. Oxford, Y.F. Wright, Jeptha Whorton, C.W. Matthews, T.M. Berry Pike. Co. I, 17th GA. Inf. was organized here August 15, 1861 by Capt. Jubilee Smith and drilled nearby.

Providence Chapel Christian Church   Circa 1857

ST. TERESA'S CATHOLIC CHURCH

Old St. Teresa's Catholic Church is located at 213 Residence Ave. in the city of Albany, GA. in Dougherty County. A new, larger parish church was dedicated in 1958 and since that time the old building has served as a second church. Presently, mass is celebrated in Spanish each week.

A GTHP marker at the site contains the following inscription:

St. Teresa's Catholic Church

St. Teresa's Church was constructed in 1859-60., on land given by Col. Nelson Tift, founder of Albany. It is the oldest church building in Albany and the oldest Catholic Church in Georgia still in use. The bricks were handmade by laborers on the Barbour Plantation near Newton. Before the interior was completed, work was halted by the outbreak of the Civil War, and for a time the church was used as a hospital for wounded Confederate soldiers.

The Church was completed after the War and, although used for Catholic worship services, it was not dedicated until 1882. On November 19 of that year, the Most Rev. William H. Gross, D.D., Bishop of Savannah, presided at the ceremony dedicating the Church under the patronage of St. Teresa of Avila. The date chosen coincided with the fiftieth wedding anniversary of John Valentine and Elizabeth Schmidt Mock, pioneer settlers of the community.

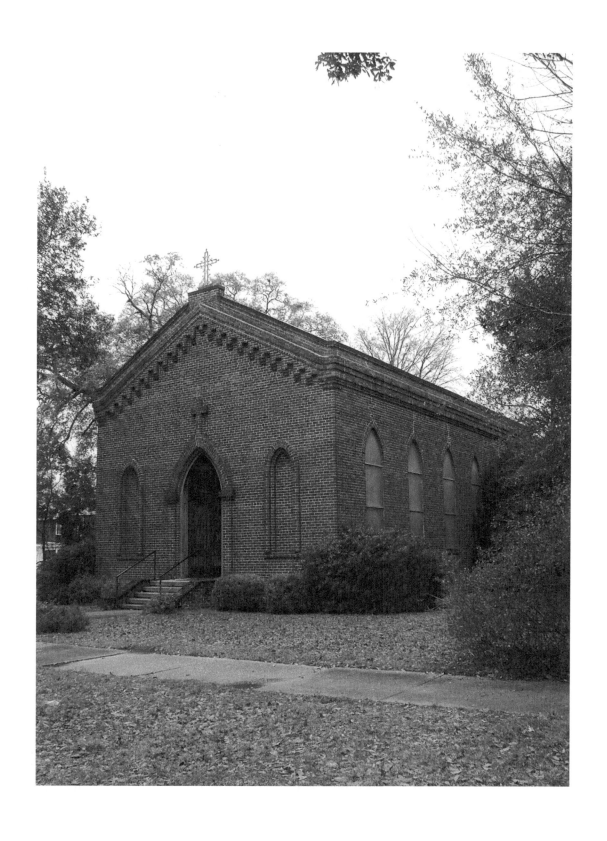

St. Teresa's Catholic Church   Circa 1859

OLD GREENFIELD CHURCH

Old Greenfield Church is located on Greenfield Church Rd. in Colquitt County, GA. There are several historic markers at this site.

The oldest marker, a marble plaque placed on an outside wall of the church over a hundred years ago by the UDC, contains the following inscription:

> *Greenfield Church. Used as a hospital and recruiting station during the War Between the States. This marker placed by Moultrie McNeil Chapter United Daughters of the Confederacy.*

A historical marker erected by the Moultrie S.C.V. contains the following inscription:

Old Greenfield Church and Historic Cemetery

> *This site, along with 19,600 acres, was purchased through a state land lottery, September, 1843-44, by Rev. Eli Graves, formerly of Vermont. In March, 1848, all was sold to his brother, Presbyterian Pastor Rev. Joel Graves. In 1850, using hand-made bricks from a nearby clay pit, Rev. Graves built the area's first brick structure, a church with annex for the area's first "common" school. The first teacher was Ruth Graves and in February, 1861, Roxanna became the second. The Post Office was at Greenfield June 26, 1856-1883. Rev. Graves brought industry to the thriving community by building a three-story building on Sloan Creek with a grist mill, general store, steam-powered wool carding factory and "bucket shop." During the War Between the States, Rev. Graves' bucket and barrel factory supplied a Confederate contract. The church served as a recruiting center and field hospital from 1863 to War's end under the care of Methodist minister and former Kentucky legislator, Rev./ Dr. Baker E. Watkins and his assistant, Dr. Samuel Hart of Americus, GA. Rev./ Dr. Watkins and Rev. Flourney Clark represented Colquitt County at the Constitution Convention of 1865. Rev./ Dr. Watkins was elected first County School Commissioner in 1872 and served in that capacity until his death in 1876.*

A plaque without attribution at the front of the church states as follows:

Old Greenfield Cemetery

> *Final resting place for Joel S. Graves, Dr. Baker E. Watkins and Elizabeth Owens Watkins, among many Confederate soldiers who died from injuries in the War.*

Old Greenfield Church   Circa 1850

EVERGREEN BAPTIST CHURCH

Evergreen Baptist Church is located on U.S. Highway 23 six miles north of the city of Cochran in Twiggs County, GA.

A GHC marker at the site has the following inscription:

Evergreen Baptist Church

Evergreen Baptist Church, built in 1844, was split off from the old Mt. Horeb Baptist Church, constituted October 5, 1809, which stood at or near the site of the Centenary Methodist Church. On February 14, 1844, the congregation and pastor found themselves locked out of church by a Brother Buckhalter. Most of the congregation, considered "Mission-minded", formed a new church, called it "Evergreen" and constructed this building in 1844. In slavery days, Negroes walked for miles to attend its services. In 1864 Negro members outnumbered White, 130 to 86.

Evergreen Baptist Church   Circa 1844

LONGSTREET METHODIST CHURCH

Longstreet Methodist Church is located on Longstreet Rd. approximately seven miles north of Cochran, GA. in Twiggs County. In 1812 the first cross state road from Augusta to Columbus was created and was called the Federal Road. That section of the road between Hawkinsville and Milledgeville was referred to as Longstreet Rd. There is no known date for the construction of the church, but the present building is the original structure and is believed to date from the early nineteenth century.

A GHC marker at the site contains the following inscription:

Longstreet Methodist Church

Longstreet Methodist Church was organized around 1812 and the original building is still in use. Land for the church was given by Charles Walker, one of the five sons of George Walker, Revolutionary soldier and early settler. The sons built on a three and a half mile stretch of the "Federal Stage and Post Road" that became known as "Longstreet". Two acres of land were given by Mr. Walker, one for the church and one for the school. The school was abandoned and its land reverted to the church. There is an old cemetery located in the rear of the church.

Longstreet Methodist Church   Circa 1825

RAMAH PRIMITIVE BAPTIST CHURCH

Ramah Primitive Baptist Church is located on Georgia Highway 57 some three miles south of the town of Gordon, GA. in Wilkinson County. The church building was constructed in 1861. A Confederate company was mustered there as part of the 7th Georgia Infantry before being sent to Lynchburg, VA. where it became attached to the 14th Georgia Infantry and became part of General "Stonewall" Jackson's famous 'Foot Cavalry'.

Community tradition recalls that Union troops camped on the church grounds in 1864 during Gen. Sherman's March to the Sea and that Union officers set up their headquarters in the church after the door locks were broken. Union forces are said to have pilfered church equipment during this occupation.

A GHC marker at the site has the following inscription:

Ramah Church

Ramah Primitive Baptist Church on the South Fork of Commissioner's Creek was constituted June 10, 1809 by the Brethren Gaylord and McGinty with ten members. Educational, social and cultural affairs of the community centered around the church for years before the town of Gordon was established. The Ramah Guards, Volunteer Infantry, C.S.A. left for Virginia from the church after impressive ceremonies and a flag presentation. Many descendants of people prominent in Ramah District still reside nearby.

The Sanders Association sponsored this marker as a memorial to the Christian spirit of Ramah's founders.

Ramah Primitive Baptist Church   **Circa 1861**

UNION CHURCH

Union Church is located at the junction of U.S. Highway 441 and Georgia Highway 57 in the town of Irwinton in Wilkinson County, GA.

Before 1854, separate buildings housed the Methodist and Baptist congregations, but during that year an arsonist, never apprehended, burned both churches as well as the county courthouse. Recognizing that the small community could not afford to rebuild both church buildings and a courthouse, the Georgia Legislature that year took an unprecedented step to charter what was called the 'Irwinton Free Church' for the purpose of housing the Methodist, the Baptist and the Presbyterian congregations.

In 1856 the present church building was erected and became known as Union Church. The designer and builder was Patrick Henry Ward, a Roman Catholic, who modeled the church after Catholic buildings of that era. By the end of the 1950's, the building was vacated and continued to deteriorate which caused a church restoration committee to be formed in 1964. The committee solicited private donations which enabled the church to be completely restored by 1966. Today it is used for special events in keeping with the three denominations that made it their home for many decades.

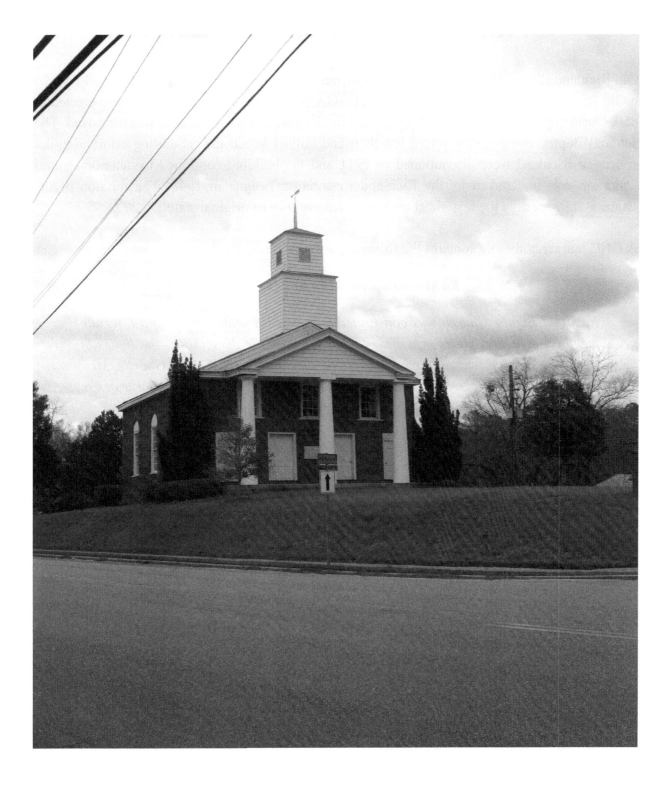

Union Church   Circa 1856

OLD RICHLAND BAPTIST CHURCH

Old Richland Baptist Church is located approximately one half mile southeast of exit 24 on I-16 on Old Richland Church Rd. in Twiggs County, GA. The present church building was erected in 1850. During the Battle of Atlanta in 1864 the First Baptist Church of Atlanta was destroyed. The Richland Baptist congregation raised ten thousand dollars to aid the rebuilding effort. Regular services at Richland were discontinued in 1911 and the building continued to deteriorate until restoration was undertaken by the Richland Restoration League in 1948. The mission of the League is "…to restore the historic church and preserve it in its original state…"

A GHC marker at the site contains the following inscription:

Richland Baptist Church

Richland Baptist Church was constituted Oct. 5, 1811 with 4 male and 8 female members. The first pastor was Rev. Micah Fulghum. In June, 1861, the ladies of this church made and presented a Confederate flag to the Twiggs Guards. Mrs. Isoline Minter Wimberly made the presentation to Sgt. Warren, color bearer of Co. I, 6th Georgia Regiment. During the war the ladies gathered in the church to prepare first aid kits.

Doors of the church closed for regular services in 1911. The Richland Restoration League, Inc. was organized in 1928 to preserve this "Landmark of Christianity."

Old Richland Baptist Church   Circa 1850

FAIRVIEW PRESBYTERIAN CHURCH

Fairview Presbyterian Church is located at 857 Duluth Hwy. in the City of Lawrenceville in Gwinnett County, GA.

Fairview Presbyterian Church was organized in 1823 under the leadership of Rev. Remembrance Chamberlain by Thomas Beattie, Samuel Reid and William Montgomery. That same year James Wardlow sold and deeded two acres to church officials at this location. The architect and builder was James S. Russell, one of the first members. It is believed construction took place in 1823.

Prior to the War Between the States the church had over 250 members, but a decline in membership occurred during the Reconstruction period. In 1907 the church was remodeled under the leadership of Rev. Fritz Rauschenberg, but the church is still situated on its original rock piers. Fairview Presbyterian is the oldest still standing church in Gwinnett County.

Fairview Presbyterian Church   Circa 1823

UNION CHAPEL METHODIST CHURCH

Union Chapel Methodist Church is located on Union Chapel Road in Putnam County, Ga. A plaque placed in front of the church by the Union Chapel United Methodist Church, Friends and the Eatonton-Putnam County Historical Society is inscribed as follows:

UNION CHAPEL UNITED METHODIST CHURCH

On April 24, 1855, Irby Hudson Scott deeded to the trustees of a newly organized and consolidated Methodist Episcopal group, three and three-quarter acres of land in Tompkins District in Putnam County, Georgia. A church building was to be erected on the land. There had been a small church on nearby land owned by the Hearn family named Bethel Church. There was also a small church named Rock Chapel on what used to be known as "the ridge road', and now called Uncle Remus U.S. Highway 441. Because the membership of each of the two churches was small, they united into one larger congregation and built a house of worship on the land offered for the purpose by Mr. Scott. These early members built well and today the building is still in excellent condition. No one now living knows where the lumber was milled but it is all the very best heart pine lumber, nowhere to be found today. The sills and framework are hand-hewn and pinned. The doors and triple-sash windows are said to have been made in Augusta, Georgia and hauled overland to the building site. The lumber used to make the pews and the door and window facing was all hand planed. The pulpit Bible was presented in 1855 and the first pastor was the Rev. Henry Morton. As early as 1867, there was a Sunday school at Union Chapel. Mr. Cullen S. Credille was superintendent of the male members and Mrs. Mary Scott was superintendent of the female members. Many years ago the orientation of the interior was changed with the pulpit and pews being reversed. Originally, the pulpit was before the high windows between the two front doors, and was mounted by steps. A new pulpit and communion rail was installed at the opposite end of the building and a center door was removed and the opening closed. On August 13, 1913, a delegation of 25 gentlemen from the Reid's Crossroad community went before the Putnam County Board of Education and requested that a better school be built in the area. The board voted to build the school at Union Chapel. The builder was Mr. Robert E. Vinning and the school was in continuous operation until county school consolidation forced its closure on May 25, 1946. The school's first teacher was Miss Fannie Mae Jones. It has been used since as Sunday school space by the church. For generations United Chapel Church and school have been important parts of the community. To those who came before us who raised the roof, stoked the fire, and kept the faith – we salute you! And to those who continue with the faith, friendship, hope and love of this body of believers – Godspeed.

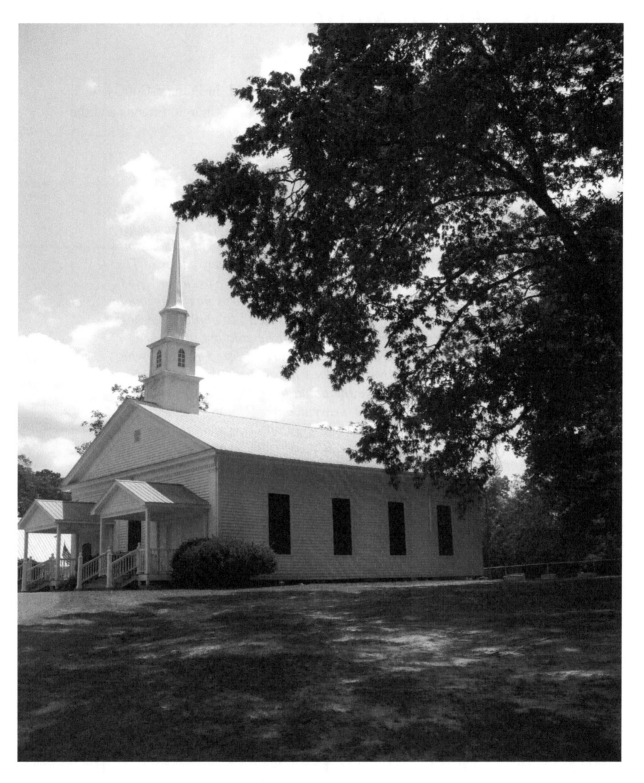

Union Chapel Methodist Church   Circa 1857

PHILADELPHIA METHODIST CHURCH

Philadelphia Methodist Church is located on New Phoenix Rd. in Putnam County, GA. A plaque placed in front of the church by Philadelphia Methodist Church, Friends and the Eatonton-Putnam County Historical Society is inscribed as follows:

PHILADELPHIA UNITED METHODIST CHURCH

In 1839, Philadelphia Sunday School Society was organized and a house of worship was built on a tract of land on Lick Creek donated by the Turner family. Joel Chandler Harris, while he lived in Turnworld Plantation, attended this church with his mentor, Joseph Addison Turner, editor of The Countryman. Near the close of the Civil War, in late November 1864, General William Tecumseh Sherman's 20th US Army Corps passed through the neighborhood on his infamous "March to the Sea" to capture the port city of Savannah for President Lincoln. Confederate soldiers who were on picket duty and camped near Philadelphia Church posted the following notice:"Soldier of the Union Army—Deface not this church, nor destroy anything within its walls as you love the union for which you are manfully fighting—An Officer." The message prevented the Union Soldiers from defacing the church building. As the congregation grew steadily after the war—its members having survived the hardship of Union-imposed post-war Reconstruction through the end of 1871—and after a more prosperous economy returned, the members of the church decided that the church building needed to be moved nearer to the center of the community. On October 15, 1884, Mrs. Frances Rhoda Hines Turner Hubert graciously deeded the land on which the present church building stands. Timbers from the original building were used in the construction of the present structure on this site. Early church records and tombstones in the large cemetery bear silent witness to the names of many early church families including Alexander, Batchelor, Beal, Credelle, Dance, Dennis, Denham, Gatewood, Holt, Little, Maddox, Montgomery, Reddick, Rogers, Rosser, Slaughter, Spivey, Turner and Wheeler. Descendents of these early families are continuing to carry on the work of the founders of this church today. This plaque is dedicated to the Glory of God and to the ministers and members of this church who have willingly given so much in order that His message of salvation and the life eternal might be shared with all mankind.

Philadelphia Methodist Church   Circa 1839

PERRY PRESBYTERIAN CHURCH

The Perry Presbyterian Church is located at 1111 Second St. in the city of Perry in Houston County, GA.

On April 25, 1847 members of the Presbyterian faith gathered in the Perry Methodist Church to form a congregation. Founding members included Dr. Charles West, Mrs. Sarah E. West, Miss Sarah West, Miss Clifford West, Dr. William S. Townshend, Mrs. Martha Townshend, Major A.W. Stephens, Mrs. Clemenia Stephens, Col. J.D. Havis, Mrs. Sophia Havis and Mr. A.A. Wilkins. The following were elected as Elders: Dr. West, Col. Havis and Dr. Townshend.

The early meetings of the congregation were held in the Baptist church in Perry. In 1849 a church building was completed. Though a larger sanctuary has been built, the original structure still serves the congregation as a fellowship hall.

Perry Presbyterian Church   Circa 1849

PERRY METHODIST CHURCH

The Perry Methodist Church is located at 1002 Carroll St. in the city of Perry in Houston County, GA.

There are two markers at this site. The first, a private marker, is inscribed as follows:

PERRY METHODIST CHURCH

ORGANIZED 1826

The first edifice was erected in 1827 on site which is now Evergreen Cemetery. The second building was located in 1846 on the front half of this square and faced Washington St.

The present sanctuary was built in 1860-61 when the other half of square was purchased. The Annex at the rear was added in 1950-51. The Educational Building was erected in 1960-61.

The exterior of sanctuary was re-modeled in 1906-07 and the interior enlarged and re-furnished in 1966-67.

The second marker, erected by the South Georgia Methodist Conference, states as follows:

PERRY
UNITED METHODIST CHURCH
1826

Organized as part of the South Carolina Conference in 1826, this church by 1830 was head of the Perry Circuit in the newly formed Georgia Conference and after 1866 in the South Georgia Conference. By 1922 Perry had become a station church. Its Sunday School, organized in 1828, has been continuous. Both the South Georgia Conference and Perry Women's Missionary Societies were organized December 15, 1879 during the 13th session of the South Georgia Annual Conference meeting in this sanctuary. Perry Ct. and Perry have given to ministry: 33 preachers, 2 deaconesses and 2 foreign missionaries in 154 years.

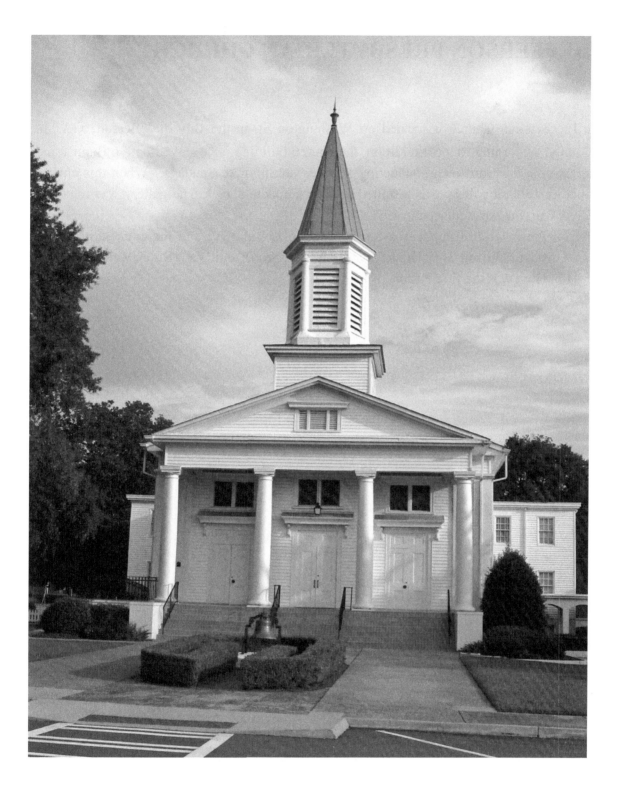

Perry Methodist Church   Circa 1860

JEFFERSON PRESBYTERIAN CHURCH

Jefferson Presbyterian Church is located on Washington St. in the City of Jefferson, GA., in Jackson County. According to local tradition, the church building once served both a Baptist and a Presbyterian congregation, each conducting services on alternate Sundays. When this church was built before 1860, a gallery was installed to accommodate slaves. The gallery was removed after the Civil War, but was replaced in 1972.

The Jefferson Presbyterian Church was formally organized in 1887 and Franklin Smith, Col. J.B. Silman, Gustavus Wilson, B.F. Hunter, Dr. Sumner J. Smith and W.G. Brock were elected as elders. Dr. H.F. Hoyt was the first Pastor.

Jefferson Presbyterian Church   Circa 1859

ANTIOCH METHODIST CHURCH

Antioch Methodist Church is located on Antioch Church Rd. in Jackson County, GA. This is a designated a United Methodist Church Historic Site and a plaque erected by the Antioch United Methodist Church Bicentennial Committee in 1999 reads as follows:

ANTIOCH UNITED METHODIST CHURCH

Antioch Church was founded in Jackson County, Georgia in 1799 on land given by the James Glenn family. The original building, along with an 1825 addition, stands to the rear of the present sanctuary forming the "T" and was bricked over in 1954 with the construction of the new building. The fellowship hall was added in 1985. The church bicentennial was held Sunday, September 12, 1999, during annual homecoming service. Antioch has been designated Historic Site number 369 by the North Georgia Annual Conference and General Commission on Archives and History of the United Methodist Church.

Many Godly pastors have served Antioch, supported by a faithful membership. As a student appointment for many years, the church nurtured young ministers, giving them the start that led to a major impact for the Kingdom of God. Many have made significant contributions to the larger church as college professors, authors, missionaries and District Superintendents.

On this hillside, the church stands as a spiritual beacon in the light of God's love and a hallowed place on holy grounds.

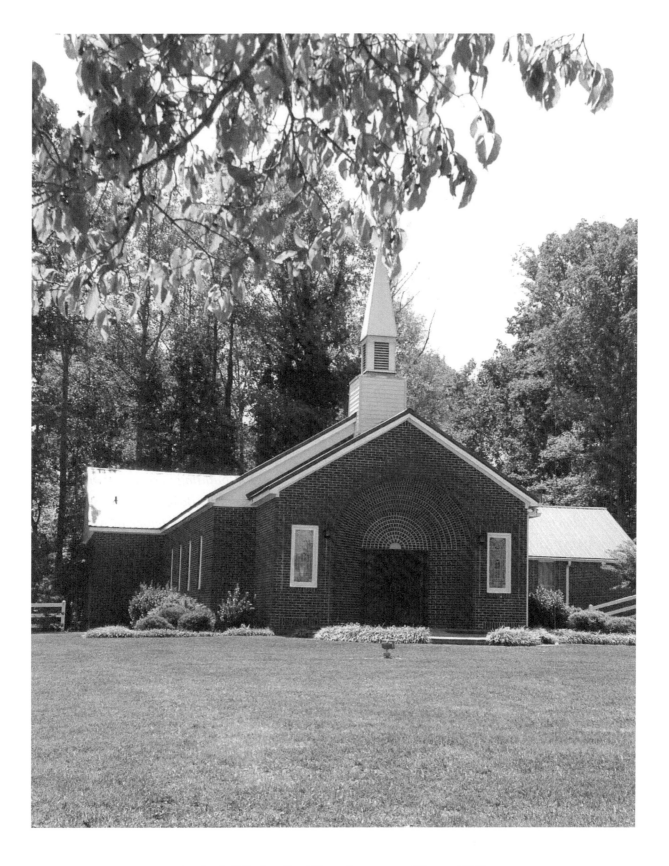

Antioch Methodist Church   Circa 1820

CARROLL'S METHODIST CHURCH

Carroll's Methodist Church is located on Carroll's Church Rd. in Franklin County, GA. This church was established in 1797. Bishop Francis Asbury preached at this site. The church building was constructed in 1835.

Two miles from the church on GA Hwy 327 is a GHC marker that contains the following inscription:

Carroll's Methodist Church

Instituted in 1797, this church was named for the William Carroll family, among its first members. Families identified with the church through the years are McWhorters, Osborns, Starrs, Stones, Browns, Burtons, Sewells, Jacksons, Hemphills, Deans, Buffingtons, Cheeks, Mabreys, Turmans, Stricklands, Carsons, Hayes, Greens, Millers and many others. The present building, erected about 1835, was restored in 1951-52 under the leadership of John H. Baker. Rev. Nelson Osborn was a lifelong member and a minister for many years. A number of well-known Georgia ministers have served the church.

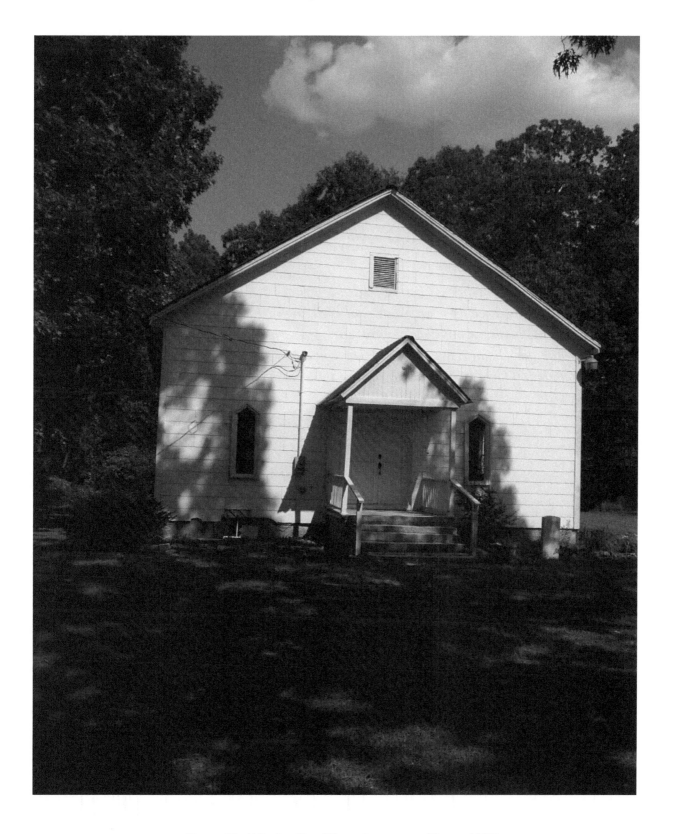

Carroll's Methodist Church   **Circa 1835**

MT. ZION CHURCH

Mt. Church is located on GA Highway 15 approximately seven miles north of Sparta, GA. in Hancock County.

A plaque attached to the church bears the following inscription:

Mt. Zion Church

The Mt. Zion Presbyterian Church was organized in 1813. $700 was raised in 1814 to complete the building. Services were held here until 1913 when the membership had dwindled to less than 10. That year the church was sold to the Methodist Church for $200.

The Methodists worshipped here until 1958. From 1958 to 1969 the Church was silent and empty, except for an occasional Wedding or Funeral. In 1969 the North Georgia Methodist Conference gave the property to the Hancock County Foundation for Historic Preservation. The combined efforts of the community and the Foundation have been made to restore this Historic old Church and preserve the records.

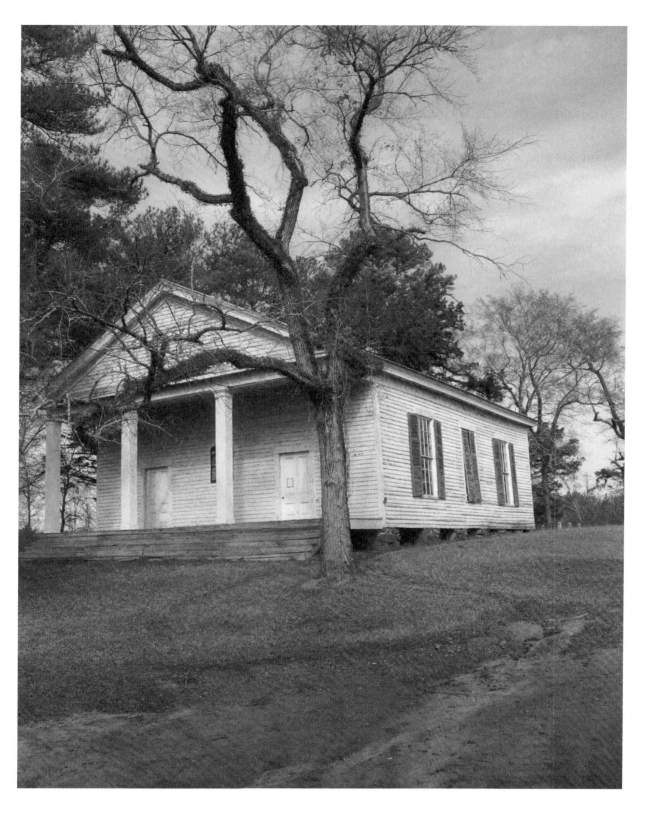

Mt. Zion Church   Circa 1814

HOPEFUL BAPTIST CHURCH

Hopeful Baptist Church is located on Winter Rd. in Burke County, GA.

A private plaque erected at the site contains the following inscription:

Hopeful Baptist Church

Hopeful was organized in October 1814 when members of the "Church at the Pinewoods Meeting House" purchased land on which the Meeting House stood for $10. The first minutes of Hopeful's history was the legal indenture recording the name "Hopeful: The Church of Christ at Hopeful met in Conference."

Built 1850-1855, costing $5,000. This 4th building of Greek Revival style is unaltered and retains its original pews, pulpit, windows, shutters, moldings.

The Church's white and black congregations worshipped together the Baptist Faith. In 1867 the black members formed the second Hopeful Baptist nearby. Still active.

The cemetery (rear) dates to 1855 with graves: Nancy Palmer Johnson (1786-1855), mother of Ga. Gov. Hershal V. Johnson, 1853-1857, Rev. V.H.T. Kilpatrick (1788-1869) and wife, Harriet. He fostered missionary sentiment and was a first trustee of Mercer University.

Edmund Byne, founder, Byne family of Burke County, was the moving force in establishing Hopeful. He died in 1814 before seeing "Fruition of his labors." Hopeful's first service was dedicated to him.

Hopeful Baptist Church was listed in the National Register of Historic Places April 1, 1993.

Hopeful Baptist Church   Circa 1850

BARK CAMP BAPTIST CHURCH

Bark Camp Baptist Church is located on Bark Camp Church Rd. four miles north of Midville in Burke County, GA. The building, closed in 1958, was restored in 2004.

A GHC marker at the site bears the following inscription:

Bark Camp Church

Constituted in the early part of 1788. Bark Camp was a center for culture and hospitality in Bark Camp, one of the oldest settlements in Burke County and a community of wealthy and prominent plantation owners. Among the 29 charter members were Miles Scarboro, Zebulon Cock and John Allen. First deacons were Zebulon Cock and probably John Allen. The first church was built of round logs: the next was of hewn logs: the third was a frame building. In 1848 a more attractive and larger building was erected.

A UDC marker affixed to the church contains the following inscription:

Bark Camp Church

Constituted in 1788. The Bark Camp Church was the center for worship, culture and hospitality in Bark Camp, one of the oldest settlements in Burke County.

Many of the congregation honorably served during the War between the States as soldiers and as members of the Ladies Volunteer Association.

General Sherman's 17th Army Corps encamped at Bark Creek Camp in December 1864.

Bark Camp Baptist Church   Circa 1848

LIBERTY METHODIST CHURCH

Liberty Methodist Church is located on Liberty Church Rd. in Hephzibah in Richmond County, GA. The building, erected in 1810, is one of the oldest Methodist churches in Georgia.

A GHC marker at the site contains the following inscription:

Liberty Methodist Church

Liberty, which evolved out of a Methodist society organized about 1775, is Georgia's oldest Methodist Church. The original log church was erected west of here by Samuel Collins who, in 1773, had emigrated from Ireland. The present church building is the third on the site and was probably erected about 1810. The first church was called Sam Collins or S.C. Church. It was begun ten years before the traditional date for the beginning of organized Methodism in Georgia. Bishop Frances Asbury visited the church March 1, 1790.

Liberty Methodist Church   Circa 1810

BATH PRESBYTERIAN CHURCH

Bath Presbyterian Church is located on Bath Edie Rd. in the town of Blythe in Richmond County, GA. Local history reveals that the town of Blythe was founded by planters and residents of Augusta and Burke County who built second homes there to escape the scourge of malaria. It is believed the present church building was constructed in 1814. A plaque affixed to the church states that the congregation was organized in 1784.

It is said that while author, clergyman and inventor the Rev. Francis R. Goulding was pastor of the church in 1842 he perfected his design of a sewing machine only to find that a similar design had only recently been submitted to the patent office.

Bath Presbyterian Church   Circa 1814

PITTS CHAPEL METHODIST CHURCH

Pitts Chapel Methodist Church is located at 132 Pitts Chapel Rd. in Jones County, GA. Church tradition maintains that on October 13, 1860, Peyton T. Pitts, Jr., a member of Clinton Methodist Church, set out to build a church on three and three fourths acres he had purchased near where Irwinton Rd. crossed Milledgeville Rd. The builder selected was a highly skilled craftsman named Owen Bostic. The church's original pulpit and pews are still in use.

The Confederate gun factory at nearby Griswoldville became a target for General Sherman's Union army in 1864. After the battle there, the church was commandeered and used as a hospital for Federal wounded.

According to the *History of the South Georgia Conference,* "The church was dedicated on August 4, 1861, by Bishop George F. Pierce, one of South Georgia's native sons."

Pitts Chapel Methodist Church   Circa 1861

ASBURY METHODIST CHURCH

Asbury Methodist Church is located on Georgia Hwy 18 in Wilkinson County near the Twiggs County line. This church was organized prior to 1850 and the building was erected in 1851 on land donated by Hardy Durham. The trustees at that time were C.G. Johnson, William M. Dennard, William Griffin, Kelly Glover and A.H. Moore.

The church was named for Bishop Asbury and early pastors were Rev. Charles G. Johnson, Rev. William Griffin, Rev. C.B.G. Johnson (the son of Rev. Charles G. Johnson.) The church building is located on the old home place of Dr. Fletcher Reed.

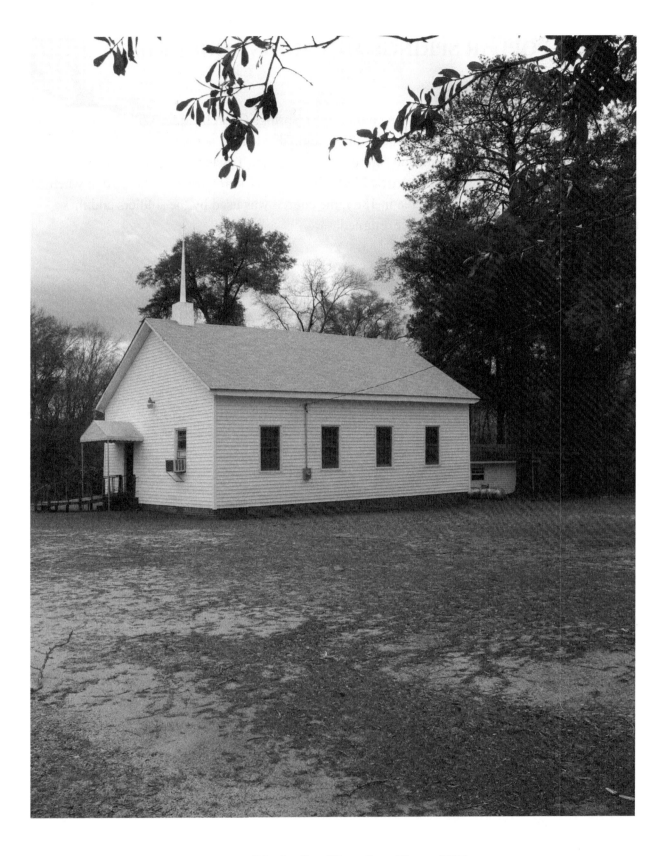

Asbury Methodist Church   Circa 1851

POPLAR SPRINGS METHODIST CHURCH

Poplar Springs Methodist Church is located on Poplar Springs Church Rd. in Wilkinson County, GA. The church was organized in 1828 and Fulton Kemp deeded ten acres to Jessie Peacock, Wiley Miller, Peter VanLandingham and Jethro Dean who were Trustees of the church.

The present church building was constructed by E.J. Tarpley. Church tradition holds that when the Union army passed through this area in 1864, the church was used by the soldiers and the church minutes were removed and never returned.

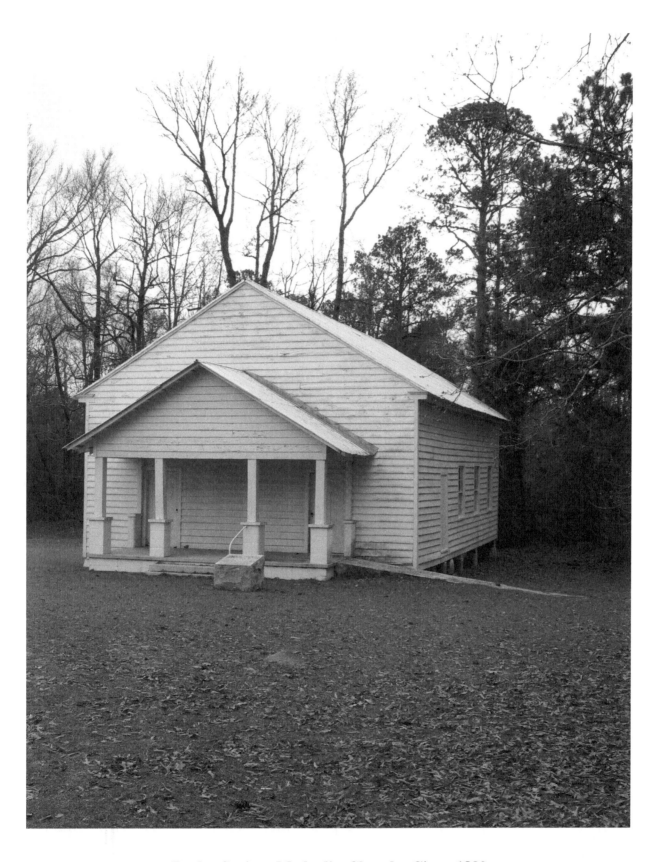

Poplar Springs Methodist Church   Circa 1830

BOILING SPRINGS METHODIST CHURCH

Boiling Springs Methodist Church is located on Boiling Springs Rd. in Laurens County, GA. According to the *History of the South Georgia Conference,* "... this church was organized in 1851 on land donated by Everard Blackshear. The pews for the church were cut on the Parson's Place and rafted down river. The pews are the originals, and each seat is made from a single plank. The floor and other essentials are also original." It is believed that the building was erected prior to the Civil War.

Boiling Springs Methodist Church   Circa 1860

DRAYTON METHODIST CHURCH

Drayton Methodist Church is located on River Road near GA Hwy 27 in the Bryomville community in Dooley County, GA.

According to the *History of the South Georgia Conference,* "When this church was built, Drayton was a village of several stores, saloon, post office and courthouse. In 1840 the present church was built …."

Drayton Methodist Church   Circa 1840

BETHEL PRIMITIVE BAPTIST CHURCH

Bethel Primitive Baptist Church is located on Bethel Church Rd. in the Pavo community in Brooks County, GA.

Local church history maintains that Old Bethel Primitive Baptist Church was constituted about a mile from its present location. Elder Matthew Albritton (1788-1850) moved his membership from Union Baptist Church (Burnt Church) to become the church's first pastor.

The present church building was constructed in 1861. The adjacent church cemetery contains the final resting place for forty seven Confederate veterans.

Bethel Primitive Baptist Church   Circa 1861

LIBERTY BAPTIST CHURCH

Liberty Baptist Church is located on Liberty Church Rd. in the Grooverville community in Brooks County, GA. Local tradition holds that the church was erected in 1859 by slaves from nearby plantations.

A GHC marker at the site bears the following inscription:

Liberty Baptist Church

Between 1837 and 1841 the Baptists in this section were stirred on missions, Sunday Schools and ministerial support. In 1841 the Ocklochnee anti-Missionary Baptist Assn. passed a ruling to dismiss members believing in the "new fangled institutions of the day." Disagreeing, Sister Nancy Hagen asked for her letter from Mt. Moriah Church and, at her request, was excommunicated. With Elisha Pack Smith, R.T. Stanaland, James I. Baker, Mrs. Sarah Ann Groover, Mrs. Mary Smith, Mrs. Amanda Denmark, and Sam Whitfield, she organized this church. The first pastor was Elder R. May. Mt. Moriah Church ceased to exist long ago.

Liberty Baptist Church   Circa 1859

GROOVERVILLE METHODIST CHURCH

Grooverville Methodist Church is located on Beasley Rd. in the Grooverville community in Brooks County, GA. No services are presently being held in the church.

A GHC marker at the site has the following inscription:

Grooverville Methodist Church

This church had its beginning in 1832, on the plantation of William H. Ramsey, about 4 ½ miles Southwest of here. There being no Methodist services in the vicinity at the time he and his family moved to this area. Mr. Ramsey built a brush arbor near his home and there held Bible study and worship services. Later he joined with other Methodist families and built a log church 3 ½ miles South on the road to St. Mark. They named this church, Lebanon, and sometime in the 1840's it was made a regular monthly appointment.

In 1856, it was decided to move the church to Grooverville, a more central location. Malachi Groover made a deed of gift of one acre of land-the present site-to Richard Ramsey, M.W. Linton and W.R. Joiner as Trustees. Mr. Linton sawed the lumber and the carpenters from his plantation built the church edifice. The name of the church was then changed to Grooverville and it became the largest on a circuit originally composed of Grooverville, Prospect, Hickory Head and Beulah. Three grandsons of Wm. H. Ramsey became Methodist ministers in the Georgia Conference.

Grooverville Methodist Church   Circa 1856

UNION PRIMITIVE BAPTIST CHURCH

Union Primitive Baptist Church, otherwise known as "Burnt Church," is located on Burnt Church Rd. near the town of Lakeland in Lanier County, GA. A local tradition holds that in 1836 a band of Creek Indians passed through this area on their way to join the Seminoles near Fargo, Fl., and set fire to the church which partially burned. The congregation then used timbers from the original building in the erection of a new church and the name "Burnt Church" reflects the use of scorched timbers in the construction.

A GHM marker near this site contains the following inscription:

Union Baptist Church

Union Baptist Church on the Alapaha River one-half mile West on this road, was constituted October 21, 1825, the first church in the old area of Irwin County.
The original members were: William A. Knight, his wife, Sarah; Jonathan Knight, his wife, Elizabeth; Joshua Lee, his wife, Martha; James Patten, his wife, Elizabeth; Mary Knight; Josiah Sirmons, deacon
The Rev. Matthew Albritton served the church as its first minister.

Union Primitive Baptist Church   Circa 1836

(Burnt Church)

BETHLEHEM PRIMITIVE BAPTIST CHURCH

Bethlehem Primitive Baptist Church is located on Bethlehem Church Rd. near the city of Quitman in Brooks County, GA.

This church was constituted about a mile from the present location in 1834. It is believed the present structure was erected in 1861.

A GHC marker located on US 221 bears the following inscription:

Bethlehem Primitive Baptist Church

Bethlehem Primitive Baptist Church, about 4 miles Southwest of here, was constituted November 29, 1834. The charter members included: William T. Rushing, his wife, Belinda; Asa Geiger, Nancy; Jared Johnson; John Turner, his wife, Lucy; Emily Turner; Henry Rowell; Cynthia Rowell; James Rowell, his wife, Jincy; Rebecca Beasley; Nellie Goff. The Rev. Ryan Frier was the first pastor; Jared Johnson and James Rowell were first deacons. The present church is about 1 mile from the original site.

Bethlehem Primitive Baptist Church   Circa 1861

SARDIS PRIMITIVE BAPTIST CHURCH

Sardis Primitive Baptist Church is located on Sardis Rd. in Charleton County, GA.

Local tradition holds that the present structure was erected around 1840. It is said that men and women sit on different sides of this church, symbolic of their equality in God's eyes.

A GHS marker located on GA Hwy 23 contains the following inscription:

Sardis Church

Sardis Church, about 2 miles west of this road, is the oldest church in Charleton County. Constituted some time before 1821, the first edifice was built in this area. The church was moved to or near its present site in 1840. The pulpit in this church has been in use for more than 100 years and bears a bullet scar from the Indian Wars. With 24 members, Sardis Church was admitted to the Alapaha River Primitive Baptist Association, October 13, 1856. In the cemetery adjacent to the church are buried many of the pioneers of this section.

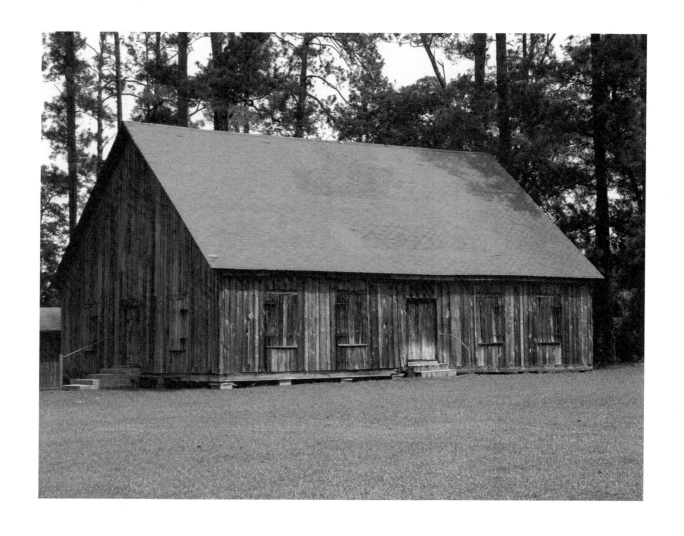

Sardis Primitive Baptist Church   Circa 1840

CAVE SPRINGS BAPTIST CHURCH

Cave Springs Baptist Church is located on Cedartown Street in the city of Cave Springs in Floyd County, Georgia.

The official computer website of Cave Springs, GA. posts the following information:

> *The Old Baptist Church was completed in 1851 and was constructed of bricks that were handmade by slaves. In the early 1930's the Baptists built another building on Cedartown Road and sold the property to Dr. J.B. Rolater. The balcony, wide plank floors, and stained glass windows make this building perfect for weddings.*

Cave Springs Baptist Church   Circa 1851

SARDIS PRESBYTERIAN CHURCH

Sardis Presbyterian Church is located on GA Highway 20 just east of the Alabama State line in the Coosa community of Floyd County, GA.

A private marker at the site contains the following inscription:

The first missionaries sent in 1821 to establish the Turnip Mountain Mission to the Cherokees was located on this site, just north of the cemetery wall. The mission, later known as Heweis, was built two miles to the east. Sardis Presbyterian Church was organized in November 1836. The first building, a log structure covered with plank, stood north of the Church. The present building was erected in 1855. The Sardis Brigade of the 6th Georgia Calvary was organized here May 9th 1861. Of the more than 235 graves in the cemetery, 18 have been identified as those of Confederate veterans. The Church became inactive in 1979 and in 1989 was deeded to the Sardis Preservation Society.

Sardis Presbyterian Church   Circa 1855

ACKNOWLEDGEMENTS

Portions of the entry "Religious Denominations in Georgia" reprinted by permission of the New Georgia Encyclopedia (www.georgiaencyclopedia.org).

Various Methodist histories and dates were verified and incorporated by permission of the South Georgia Conference Commission on Archives and History for the Bicentennial of American Methodism. *History of the South Georgia Conference, The United Methodist Church 1866-1984.* Dallas: Taylor Publishing, 1984.

Portions of the entries "Historical Markers in the State of Georgia" and "Early Christian Footprints in Georgia" reprinted by permission of Joiner, Don. *Antebellum Churches in Georgia.* Raleigh: Lulu Press, 2007.

CPSIA information can be obtained at www.ICGtesting.com
Printed in the USA
LVOW010603140113

315590LV00004B/7/P